PICKPOCKETS

Keep Wall Street Out of Your Pocket and End Up with More.

STEPHEN R. BECK • MITCHELL TUCHMAN

EDITED BY MILLER MCMILLAN

Published by White Hat Publishing

ISBN: 0615608310
ISBN 13: 9780615608310

Dedication

This book is dedicated to John Bogle, Charles Ellis, Burton Malkiel, Harry Markowitz, David Swensen, William Bernstein, Eugene Fama and William Sharpe.

They've blown Wall Street's cover with heaps of research; they've conclusively demonstrated that low-cost indexing beats active management by a long shot; and they proved that the buy, hold, and rebalance style of investing trumps the vein-popping practices of Jim Cramer and crew.

Their courageous and pioneering work has done immeasurable good for retirement investors worldwide.

We thank you.

About PickPockets

Most people think they need to play by Wall Street's rules in order to grow their investments. Surprise. Wall Street may be the worst thing for your future.

PickPockets shows you the pitfalls of the Wall Street game and how many brokers, money managers and investment advisers are experts at picking your pocket. *This book* is a compilation of short blog posts written by financial experts Mitch Tuchman and Stephen Beck and distributed to thousands of investors on the authors' online investment site, MarketRiders (www.marketriders.com).

Tuchman and Beck show you why the world's wealthiest families and elite institutions such as Yale and Harvard ignore Wall Street. The stories are easy to read, laced with humor, and brimming with practical insights that will educate and inspire individual investors.

Be prepared. This style of investing will not fire up the adrenal glands, trigger manic trading, fuel your need for daily entertainment, or support the illusion of having a stock and bonds crystal ball. But it just might change your investment habits forever and redefine your retirement years for the better.

PickPockets Helps Every Investor: From Doctors, Pastors, Engineers, and Designers to CEOs

"I was a Wall Street analyst at Goldman Sachs and Citibank and I know how tough it is to do better than the markets. Friends used to ask what to do for investing and now I tell them to just read PickPockets and do what Steve and Mitch are preaching. It works!"

Tom Berquist
CEO, Corel Software

"Over the years, I interviewed many investment experts on KGO News Talk 810 AM. When Mitch and Steve joined my program, the lines jammed up. The response was overwhelming. Their method is proven, thought provoking, intelligent and struck a positive chord that continues to resonate far and wide. If you value your money, you must read this book."

John F. Rothmann
Talk Show Host

"I was tired of being talked down to by brokers and financial advisors. PickPockets completely demystified investing for me. I've got all I need to know about investing so that I can make sure my retirement accounts will take care of me when I need them."

Jessica Weil
Susie Fox Jewelry

"My 401k was sitting at my old employer doing nothing. PickPockets gave me tools to start doing things myself and I feel like I'm now in control."

Maurice Berdugo
Partner, BP Analytics

"Successful portfolio management is a dance between risk, return, and cost. Risk and return make great dance partners while cost is the obnoxious drunk who tries to butt in. Investing becomes a beautiful thing when the drunk gets booted from the party. Mitch and Steve are great bouncers. Heed their advice and you'll be dancing with the stars in no time!"

Rick Ferri, CFA
Author and Founder, Portfolio Solutions, Inc.

"We've helped place over 1000 consultants and contractors, many of whom have to figure out their own retirement plans. PickPockets is invaluable for anyone who wants to maximize their nest egg!"

Cara France
CEO, The Sage Group

"I was an investment banker at Salomon Brothers for 10 years, led the management led buyout of one of the world's largest technology companies-- which I now run. In all my varied experience with investing, I have found the contents of PickPockets to be the single best, consistent advice on investment strategy I've come across."

Steve Luczo
Chairman and CEO, Seagate Corporation

"Most corporate directors clearly understand and abide by our fiduciary responsibility to shareholders. Too bad many in the investment advisory business don't. PickPockets helped me spot advisers who put their interests ahead of mine."

Betsy Atkins
Director at Polycom, SunPower, Chicos, Schneider Electric

"I was so confused by the process and so weary of working with guys on commission, that I became paralyzed and didn't do anything. PickPockets' impressive collection of insights helped me cut through the myths. I now have a better understanding of the right way to invest. My conundrum is over!"

Todd Brinton, MD
Cardiologist & Clinical Associate Professor Stanford University

"As a pastor, I need to make the most of my retirement account. I held a number of mutual funds for years only to see my portfolio dwindle under the weight of heavy fees. PickPockets gave me the confidence to go it alone and I've never looked back!"

Rev. Sean Blomquist
Pastor, Shelter Covenant Church

Table of Contents

Introduction

The rich invest differently. They use a little-known method that Wall Street intentionally conceals. Wealthy families, pension fund and endowment managers have used this method for decades to compound their already staggering wealth. All the while, average investors scurry about in search of the next crumb of stock that will become their ticket to paradise.

PickPockets shows you a better way to invest. The book is a compilation of short articles penned by financial experts Mitch Tuchman and Stephen Beck over the past few years. The posts were distributed to thousands of investors on U.S. News and World Report (www.usnews.com) and those who subscribe to the authors' online investment website, MarketRiders (MarketRiders.com). The articles explain how the average investor gets pickpocketed and how the wealthy make—and keep—more money.

Wall Street keeps this wealth-building method hidden from everyday investors because if it were discovered and employed, money management firms would lose billions of dollars in profits. By reading this book, you position yourself to not only become informed, but to be counted among the liberated. You will learn the MarketRiders philosophy of how to pull your dollars away from ineffectual fee takers and keep it where it belongs—growing in your account.

The story of MarketRiders is really the story of Mitch Tuchman and Steve Beck, two Silicon Valley entrepreneurs and investors whose journeys led them to the discovery of this hidden methodology. In turn, they did what they do best—transform good ideas into easily used software, initially for the benefit of friends and family. Little did they know that word-of-mouth recommendations and eventually media interest would lead to the launch of their software-enabled website, MarketRiders

MarketRiders has liberated thousands of investors who now easily employ the practices of the wealthy from the comfort of their own homes. These investors have kept billions of dollars of investment capital from the fetters of Wall Street fees. Their pockets are no longer picked.

The idea began in the fertile mind of Mitch Tuchman, the founder of MarketRiders. Mitch had just finished a season of institutional money management at a leading long-short hedge fund, where he was responsible for several hundred-million-dollar portfolios of small capitalization US stocks. Through rigorous research, cutting-edge information systems, and management tools, Mitch had become aware of the difficulty of outperforming the US small-cap index, even with the advantage of expert knowledge at his disposal.

Mitch was also interacting with leading endowment and pension managers who were investors in his hedge fund. He became privy to the approach being used by big-money investors—what we now call the MarketRiders methodology. These investors were not focused on stock picking, but on a sophisticated and disciplined investment strategy rooted in decades of scientific study. This strategy focuses on spreading investments globally across low-correlated asset classes, aggressively keeping fees low, and staying true to target allocations through consistent rebalancing.

As these newly learned investment insights were percolating in Mitch's mind, he was confronted with the sobering task of overseeing the management of a modest trust fund set up to address the lifelong needs of a disabled cousin. It is difficult enough for a retirement investor to trust his hard-earned dollars to an investment strategy, especially in times like these. It is quite another thing to be entrusted with the fiduciary responsibility to provide for the lifelong needs of a vulnerable relative. Coincidentally, Mitch's father approached him for help managing his retirement account. A very successful entrepreneur, Mitch's father was weary of the aggressive pitches he was hearing from the big wealth managers.

With these mandates, Mitch began his research. He studied the underlying financial theories behind leading endowments and pensions. His efforts led him to several dozen books and articles by such authors as John Bogle, founder of the Vanguard Group; David Swensen, Chief Investment Officer of the Yale Endowment; investment icons Charles Ellis and Dr. Burton Malkiel; and the academic writings of Nobel Prize–winning Dr. William Sharpe of Stanford, Dr. Eugene Fama of the University of Chicago, and many others.

During his research into institutional money management, Mitch uncovered a little-known investment secret. Mitch spun a sophisticated spreadsheet that would allow him and his friends to use this secret and implement an investing system. After tweaking the spreadsheet, he quickly realized that a streamlined version would be better, so he hired engineers to take his idea online and implement a friendlier interface.

One of the first people he showed his work to was his longtime friend and former business associate Stephen Beck. Steve and Mitch had been partners in a technology company in the late 1990s and had sold the company to Inktomi, the pre-Google global leader in Internet search.

Steve's journey as an investor was the opposite of Mitch's. While Mitch branched off into the investment business after the sale of their company, Steve entered the world of money management via a boutique Silicon Valley venture capital firm. Through a fortuitous set of events, Steve found himself leveraging his Internet search experience to not only invest in what would become the largest technology company in China, but also to help operationally as an active member of Baidu's board of directors.

Steve sorted through a myriad of approaches to wealth management. Like many who work hard to save, Steve had developed expertise in his industry but knew little about actual wealth management. He turned to the leading wealth management firms for help and was quickly swept into the Wall Street machine. Wealthy Silicon Valley friends told him of a top-notch wealth manager at Lehman Brothers who, based on their recommendation, might be able to take him on. You can guess the pitch: an elite team of money mangers, the best research, access to inside deals, and, yes, high fees—in exchange for mind-blowing returns.

The scarcity pitch worked perfectly. Steve felt privileged to have his money in the care of Lehman's elite team. A few years later, the technology bubble burst and Lehman's active management methodology resulted in the evaporation of close to half of Steve's net worth. Indeed, his mind was blown, but in a way he had never imagined.

Fortunately, with Baidu's success, Steve still had money to invest. He was determined not to make the same mistake again, so he began a rigorous process of interviews to find a firm he could truly trust. Each firm had a compelling twist on the same active money-management tale—market-beating performance via the firm's unique advantage. Steve figured that his job was to identify an outstanding team that was impeccably trustworthy, intelligent, and skilled at their work. As is the case with most investors, it never occurred to him that the active money-management game is a failed business—a Wall Street version of the *The Wizard of Oz*—that lacks the magic it portends.

Unfortunately, it took another round of disappointment at the hands of a leading firm before Steve took a step back to examine the very assumptions of Wall Street—that high fees and active management actually work. It was in this context that his path again crossed with Mitch's. Mitch shared his reading list with Steve, who quickly learned the investment practices of the truly wealthy. Mitch and Steve joined forces and MarketRiders was born.

Whether you are like Mitch, a researcher who discovered the MarketRiders methodology before he lost any money, or like Steve, who had to reexamine the fundamental assumptions of wealth management, this book presents an opportunity to join the revolution of "money out of management." Stand on the shoulders of the authors and give your portfolio the advantage of their methodology—without committing to months of research or paying a small fortune for advice. Within these pages is the best investment advice you will otherwise never hear. Wall Street bigwigs won't be happy you're reading these pages, but you'll be glad you did.

PART ONE

How Your Pocket Gets Picked

CHAPTER 1

Are You Gambling or Investing?

"It's like giving up a belief in Santa Claus. Even though you know Santa Claus doesn't exist, you kind of cling to that belief. I'm not saying that Wall Street is a scam. They want to believe they can beat the market. The evidence is, however, that they can't."

—BURTON MALKIEL, PRINCETON UNIVERSITY

Wall Street is about activity—buying, selling, commissions, fees, listening to the "pros," beating the "house," and "don't try this at home." But does all this activity really help you as an investor? Many money managers do beat the market in a given year, and maybe even for several years. But as happens in a casino, where the odds are stacked against you, the vast majority of fund managers eventually fail. Meanwhile, they earn their fees regardless of how they perform. And by making investing look complicated and scary, they keep you at their table. Are you a gambler or an investor? This chapter shows you the difference.

Choosing an Investment Game You Can Win

(MAY 29, 2010)

There are different types of retirement investors and, ultimately, different approaches to growing your money. Some investors play the high stakes game of competing against the market itself. These investors have entered the largest poker tournament the world has to offer. Who joins these gamblers at the table? Teams of the smartest minds, best researchers, and leading technologists backed by shockingly large coffers—Wall Street professionals who are in it to win.

Investors who enter this tournament via day trading, market timing, technical analysis, or even tactical asset allocation need to pay close attention. They are playing a game that is very difficult to win, especially if they have few resources, little knowledge, and less technology than the competition. Oh, sure, they might be lucky enough to win a few early hands, but the long-term outcome is fairly predictable. Such investors live with a prevailing sense of unrest knowing that they are showing up to a shotgun duel with nothing more than a pocketknife.

WHAT DO THE WEALTHY KNOW?

Wealthy families, endowment managers, and elite institutions practice a different investment approach. These investors are wise enough to avoid paying fees to managers trying to beat the averages in public stock markets. They may invest in private equity and venture capital funds, in which they enjoy access to the best deals and terms, but when it comes to public markets, they commit a large portion of their portfolios to passive indexed strategies—the MarketRiders approach. The only bet such investors make is that the world is not coming to an end any time soon and that its markets, companies, and portfolios will continue to grow over long periods of time.

This approach provides an investor with freedom from having to stare at his or her portfolio several times a day. Unconcerned with the daily gyrations of Jim Cramer and the rest of the bobblehead finance media, long-term and disciplined MarketRiders can go about their daily lives with peace of mind. The market was down in May and investors' portfolios probably dropped with it, but with a retirement time horizon that is years away, their portfolios will not only recover, but will also grow quite nicely. By rebalancing, these investors are taking advantage of swings. This knowledge frees them from staring at computers and gives them time to go about the real business of living life. In the end, isn't that what money is for?

Are You the House or the Drunken Guest?

(SEPTEMBER 1, 2011)

Are you saving money to travel, buy things you want, help charities and people you love, send kids to college, stop working—or just plain relax? If so, consult your favorite Wall Street broker or mutual fund manager, or become a stock picker yourself. Either way, within twenty years, you'll be saying goodbye to 33 percent of your money and many of your dreams.

HOW ACTIVITY HURTS

How could this be true? The answer is simple. Most people confuse investing with gambling. Gamblers try to beat the house. Investors want to *be* the "house."

Imagine a casino in Las Vegas called World Markets. This casino offers many gaming options—blackjack, poker, roulette, craps, and slots—along with great food, entertainment, and well-appointed rooms.

Guests have a lot of fun at World Markets, thrilled by the excitement of gambling and the highs and lows of winning and losing. Some approach the table with various systems to beat the house, such as statistical models and card counting. Others talk to God.

A grandmother dropped a quarter in a slot machine and won $250,000. A guest who had never played blackjack hit twenty-one on his first hand, made $50,000, and proposed to and married his girlfriend—all in one night.

World Markets Casino is exciting, to be sure. Any doubts, just look at the brochures.

A GAME THAT'S HARD TO WIN

Most guests don't just play, win, and leave, however. They *keep* playing, and that's what World Markets counts on. Like all casinos, it has special house odds. Sooner or later World Markets will win more money than it loses, thanks to human nature and statistics. Depending on the game and how wagers are placed, the casino will earn commission of up to 35 percent from the winnings. It is impossible to do consistently, but guests come back year after year in hopes of beating the house.

A BETTER APPROACH FOR YOUR MONEY

Here lies the hard and fast difference between an investor and a gambler: investors care about only one thing—making money. They're not concerned with having fun or reminiscing about the night they had hot dice at the craps table. They couldn't care less if they never heard the *ka-ching* of a winning pull at a slot machine. They just want to know that they'll make money year after year.

Suppose you buy stock in the imaginary World Markets, Inc. (WMKTS). WMKTS investors never know from night to night where they'll make money. Some nights they might lose to a guest with a streak of luck on the craps table, but the next night, WMKTS might make money on blackjack.

WMKTS INVESTORS ARE THE "HOUSE"

By spreading the risk among several "games" and not getting caught up in greed and other emotions, investors make more money investing in the house instead of trying to beat it. It's just a statistical fact.

So how is it that most people invest their money as if they were gambling in WMKTS rather than investing in it?

Most investors attempt to beat the house in world asset markets—US stocks, bonds, real estate, foreign stocks, and emerging market stocks—by picking stocks on their own, giving money to a broker who they believe is a good stock picker, or investing in a mutual fund with a great track record.

THE PRICE OF TRYING TO BEAT THE HOUSE

Years of studies confirm that investors do worse than the house by spending money trying to beat it. Investors leave an average of 2 percent of their funds with trusted advisers and pay higher taxes because buying and selling stocks creates taxable income. Due to mathematical laws such as compound returns, investors can lose 33 percent of their money over twenty years—just like a guest at World Markets Casino.

How do you become an investor in WMKTS instead of a gambler? By buying and holding a collection of exchange-traded funds (ETFs).

For every $100,000 invested, you'll pay $200 in yearly fees instead of $2,000 to money managers, financial advisers, and broker commissions. Invest the way smart investors and endowment managers do at Yale, Harvard, Princeton, and Stanford. You'll never have to pick a stock or mutual fund again, and you can dial the risk levels of your portfolio up or down to suit your comfort level.

Be the house, not the guest.

Being Smart Instead of Busy in Your Investing

(JUNE 5, 2010)

Do you like investing? Do you find it fun to study investment resources to better your investing habits? Have you given your children a few bucks to buy their favorite stocks so they can start early and learn important financial lessons?

You may be wasting your time. And worse, becoming an active investor may not be good for your financial health. Unless you are a hyperkinetic trader with a true edge on Wall Street, one of the paradoxes of investing is that activity has little or no correlation with success. In fact, more activity often leads to bad results.

Active investing is about being right, not about what you do. Warren Buffett has two great quotes on this aspect of investing: "Much success can be attributed to inactivity" and "Most investors cannot resist the temptation to constantly buy and sell."

"Nobody Knows Nothing"

(APRIL 24, 2010)

Screenwriter William Goldman made this statement about the movie business. He meant that even after more than one hundred years of movie making, no one actually knows how to make a successful movie. Sometimes sure things bomb; sometimes long shots win big.

To draw a parallel, we often assemble indisputable studies that describe how random investment success really is. For example, if you own actively managed mutual funds, you'll retire with a lot less money than if you'd bought, held, and rebalanced the boring ETFs that we and others recommend. This is a fact that's been proven over and over again.

Why do so many investors want to believe something that isn't true? Ivy League MBAs who are smart, motivated, and hardworking can surely beat a dumb computer managing an ETF or index, right? Wrong—for two reasons. First, investment pros charge fees that are an impossible handicap. Second, unlike other professions (surgeon, litigator, racecar driver, or pilot, for example) in which success can be accounted for by how well one manages risk, most professional investors who beat the market in a given year are just plain lucky. They win for short periods of time because of random events, not skill or intelligence. Just luck. We became acutely aware of this fact in 2008 when none of the gurus predicted what was about to happen to the economy.

Consider it likely that great professional investors may be no better off than the four finalists in the eighth round of a thousand-monkey coin-flipping contest. Yes, there will always be a winner. But why does the winner win? Does someone know something? Or is it monkey business?

Can You Compete Against 1 Billion IQ Points?

(FEBRUARY 19, 2011)

While you sit on your couch watching the dizzying array of securities prices on CNBC, there are many forces at work in the background. All day every day, thousands of experienced, educated investors from around the globe work to find inefficiencies in the prices of everything from stocks in Egypt to municipal bonds in California.

They research every security in the world, from Dell Computers and Japanese debt to euros, gold, and pork bellies. They often know more about a company than the management teams running them. They rarely take vacations. Armed with the most expensive computing equipment in the world, they pore over data to figure out what a particular security is worth.

They set up Google alerts to receive incremental updates from remote bloggers. They hire private investigators to check sell-through prices of products at retail. Some will stop at nothing to find the slightest edge. Recently, several hedge fund managers were arrested for insider trading because they paid moles inside public companies to give them information that others didn't have.

IS YOUR GUESS AS GOOD AS THEIRS? THINK AGAIN

Based on this research, they form opinions and bet billions of dollars on what they think will happen. They trade. They agree on a price. The buyer thinks an upside exists and the seller doesn't believe there is enough upside—or he's lost so much that he can't take it. Prices change in a nanosecond based on incremental, seemingly infinitesimal data, such as Steve Jobs's health, a protest in Yemen, or even a bug found on an Intel chip.

You can think whatever you want about the price of bonds, gold, or US stocks, but these investors have already thought about it, their computers have thought about it, and they've bid against one another to determine whether they are buyers or sellers. All of these elements are factored into the price you see.

WHAT TO DO? OWN ETFS

Equipped with this knowledge, what do the smartest investors do? They own a little of everything in proportions that make sense for their individual situations, remembering that in the next year, some of their holdings will rise and others will fall. Smart investors own stocks from the United States through funds such as Vanguard Total Stock Market ETF (VTI) and from around the world through funds such as VGK and VPL. They own bonds through Vanguard Total Bond Market ETF (BND), get commodities exposure through SPDR Gold Shares (GLD) or iShares S&P Global Energy (IXC), and get real estate exposure in an ETF fund such as RWR. They have the discipline to trim what is going up and buy what is going down. These investors bought more stocks and trimmed their bond holdings when the S&P fell below seven hundred in March 2009. Today, they're adding to their bonds and trimming their stocks.

You have two choices as a retirement investor. You can have faith that capital markets will grow over time and generate a reasonable return without knowing where those returns will come from in a given year, or you can actively shift your money around like a kid avoiding obstacles in a car racing video game.

In the end, the first choice yields tranquility, and the second, heart palpitations. Don't fight against the billion IQ points. Own a bit of everything.

What a Fool Believes

(NOVEMBER 13, 2010)

On their 1978 album *Minute By Minute,* the Doobie Brothers tell the tale of a man who believes a lie of his own fabrication. Somehow, this poor sap convinced himself that he is a Casanova, the apple of some woman's eye, when in fact he was never so much as a blip on her radar.

This fictitious character's predicament is not much different from what many retirement investors face. They are in love with the Wall Street fantasy of trouncing the markets through laser-sharp equity selection. Many prefer to see themselves as clones of Warren Buffett, their glasses slung low on the bridge of their nose while they astutely gaze past today's *Journal* to process terabytes of random data in search of the investment insight of the day.

Are you living this Wall Street fantasy? You are not alone. Millions of investors share that perspective and believe what a fool believes. Let's look at the truth about Wall Street and how beating the market is virtually impossible.

GETTING REAL

It's a fact: research unequivocally shows that only a tiny percentage of professional money managers display extraordinary talents. For those who value facts over fantasy, the fulcrum about which all investment activity should turn is the fact that an overwhelming majority of active money managers do not beat the market.

Research by CXO Advisory Group LLC reveals that stock-market gurus have an average forecasting accuracy rate of 47.5 percent in any given year. You would do better flipping a coin. A closer look at the stats is even more interesting: by extending the investment time horizon to five years, only one in three active managers beats his or her index. For the betting man, these odds are unacceptable.

What if you tried to game the system and bought only top performing, actively managed funds, as the Morningstar systems seem to suggest? Within five years, 20 percent of these top-performing funds would be closed due to poor performance, and 83 percent would underperform against the index. Wow!

THE NUMBERS DON'T LIE

These facts relate to one fund in one asset class. What happens if we apply active management to a real-world scenario in which your time horizon is ten years out and you are actively investing across six or more asset classes? What are your odds of beating the market? Research puts this likelihood below five percentage points.

As one famous money manager, Bill Gross of PIMCO, bravely stated, "The industry as a whole cannot outperform the market because they are the market, and long-term statistics revealing negative alpha for the class of active managers confirms it. Yet, what a price investors are willing to pay!"

So what does a fool believe? Among other things, that he can do what professional managers cannot—beat the market. For those who prefer reality, low-cost indexing, asset allocation, and driving down all unnecessary fees are the game of the day. We, too, enjoy reading our daily *Journal*, but we have been schooled by the facts and are better for it.

Tsunamis, Nukes, and Uprisings: Why Smart Investors Don't Predict

(MARCH 19, 2011)

The year 2011 began with a series of cataclysmic events that rattled the world and sent markets into mental states not yet diagnosed by the field of psychiatry. How did you react?

This year has been full of the unexpected. The world is an unpredictable place. It was only a few weeks ago that Egypt and then Libya dominated the airwaves. Now they are distant memories after the horrific events in Japan this week. Who would have thought that an earthquake would lead to a nuclear meltdown? Who would have predicted that Arab dictatorships would topple because of Facebook and Twitter? What is an investor to do?

The answer lies in whether your investment focus is based on predicting or positioning. It's a lot more fun to invest based on predictions. Jim Cramer and the pundits interviewed on CNBC are highly entertaining. They tell us with utmost certainty what will happen with a company, a sector, or an economy. And they know how to provoke our fear and greed so that we'll keep watching.

FORGET CRYSTAL BALLS

Most everyday investors only know an investment world based on predictions. They've heard about the mutual fund manager who finds undervalued companies by predicting cash flows, the Merrill Lynch broker who calls with his analyst's latest tip, the Motley Fool newsletters, and the UBS economist who predicts a drop in the US dollar. But most of us are still smarting over portfolios damaged by the 2008 financial meltdown, which forecasters failed to predict.

Another group of investors—institutional investors such as pension, endowment, and foundation managers—believe that predicting the future is at best informed fortune telling. After decades of research and experience, they've concluded that it's better to focus on being positioned instead of attempting to predict what will happen in the world. They know there are risks that can't be articulated or imagined, let alone predicted, so they endeavor to build portfolios that will withstand the unexpected.

Most institutional investors have fully recovered from the 2008 meltdown. They didn't sell stocks in a panic in March 2009—they bought them. What can we learn from them?

STAY THE COURSE

First, institutional investors face sobering tasks. Pension plan managers must send checks to retirees every month. Managers of university endowments must help pay for scholarships and faculty salaries. They want portfolios with a variety of assets that behave differently depending on the scenario. They reason through allocations to US stocks, Treasuries, foreign stocks, real estate, or commodities. When the world panics, investors flock to Treasuries. When inflation worries are front and center, commodities and real estate benefit at the expense of Treasuries.

They debate these issues and end up with a policy that can only be changed by committee. Once they agree on the policy, they look for the best ways to get exposure for each type of asset. They focus on fees. They only hire managers if they feel they can outperform; otherwise, they buy index funds. They don't care about Netflix or Apple. They care about whether they have the right allocation to US growth stocks. And when the markets undergo big changes and the actual percentages differ from their original recipes, they don't panic. They don't change their policy. They rebalance to it. These investors are probably buying Japanese companies this week because their allocations have changed since the recent earthquake.

POSITION, DON'T PREDICT

There is a quiet but growing revolution going on in American retirement investing. Baby boomers are ready to retire and they don't have enough money. They've grown weary of expensive predictions. They want to be positioned. Earthquakes, tsunamis, and revolts become stress tests for how well a portfolio is positioned. Was your portfolio well positioned over the past six weeks? Are you trying to predict what will happen next? Think about positioning, not predicting, and manage your family money the way the smart guys do.

What Wall Street Doesn't Want You to Know

(MARCH 26, 2011)

Have you ever met a crazy conspiracy theorist who is convinced that a well-executed and malevolent plot lurks behind most events? These were the people whose eyes bugged out during Y2K, who are convinced that Apollo 11 never landed on the moon, and who thought that the World Trade Center was blown up by the United States to garner support for invading the Middle East. The conspiracy thread has woven a thick yarn throughout the ages. It would be worthy of a good laugh if it weren't for the sick feeling you get when you realize that some people actually believe that stuff.

There is one conspiracy worthy of your attention, however. Those on Wall Street don't want you to know that their industry is a sham. The hypnotic malaise they cast over the unknowing investor is nothing less than an $11-trillion shell game. Their gambit makes the baccarat table at the Bellagio look like a neighborhood lemonade stand.

Like any good shell game, they keep the pea moving so you never really understand what's happening. Hideous mutual funds vanish into thin air so that fund companies can claim that their winning funds are leaping tall indexes in a single bound. High fees slip out from your account while you sleep peacefully, believing they have your back. What about the media? Reports are so convoluted that you have to be a Nobel Laureate in economics to figure out what you made—or lost—after fees and taxes in a given year. Did you know that it nearly took an act of Congress to force 401(k) providers to tell employees in plain language how much they pay in fees?

WHO ELSE IS SKEPTICAL OF WALL STREET?

Speaking of Nobel Laureates, fortunately a few have been paying attention: Harry M. Markowitz, Merton H. Miller, William F. Sharpe, and Charles Ellis, along with Nobel candidate Eugene Fama and other notable luminaries such Princeton professor and author Burton Malkiel; John Bogle, founder of Vanguard; and William Bernstein, the acerbic author and truth teller. If you haven't yet familiarized yourself with their findings, the time has come to do so. They've blown Wall Street's cover with heaps of research; they've conclusively demonstrated that low-cost indexing beats active management by a long shot; and they proved that the buy, hold, and rebalance style of investing trumps the vein-popping practices of Jim Cramer and crew.

But the good guys' PR campaign is weak. While they stutter in the corner, Wall Street spews out eloquent waves of hypnotic media that roll over us in a tsunami of minute-long TV ads, billboard artistry, and heart-grabbing radio spots. Each makes you want to pull out your hanky, pick up the phone, and call your mom to tell her you love her.

DISCERNMENT TO THE RESCUE

Who cares about facts when Smith Barney speaks? What about the TD Ameritrade guy, Sam Waterston? He played stalwart Jack McCoy on the NBC series *Law & Order.* He sure cracked the code there, so he'll be the guy I can trust for my retirement, right?

Yes, there are excellent online brokers. For a fair, low price, you can have excellent trade execution and fulfillment and receive tremendous customer service and online reporting. But watch your pocket if you go to brokers for investment advice. Chances are they will roll out the four-color glossy print, begin a full-court press, and slip you right into some mutual funds that drip, drip, drip away your hard-earned savings in high fees and underperformance.

Conspiracy theories are for the birds. Ours, however, isn't one of them. Facts are for the discerning. When it comes to Wall Street, the facts have been revealed by the best economic minds in the world. Are you listening?

Experts Speak

"The deeper one delves, the worse things look for actively managed funds."

—DR. WILLIAM BERNSTEIN, AUTHOR

"Most investors are pretty smart. Yet most investors also remain heavily invested in actively managed stock funds. This is puzzling. The temptation, of course, is to dismiss these folks as ignorant fools. But I suspect these folks know the odds are stacked against them, and yet they are more than happy to take their chances."

—JONATHAN CLEMENTS, ECONOMIST

"It turns out there is no such thing as stock picking skill. It's human nature to find patterns where there are none and to find skill where luck is a more likely explanation (particularly if you're the lucky mutual fund manager). We are looking at the proverbial bunch of chimpanzees throwing darts at the stock page. Their 'success' or 'failure' is a purely random affair."

—DR. WILLIAM BERNSTEIN, AUTHOR

"In a New York Times contest, funds chosen by advisors performed 40 percent less than the index."

—JOHN BOGLE, FOUNDER OF THE VANGUARD GROUP

"If there's ten thousand people looking at the stocks and trying to pick winners, one in ten thousand is going to score, by chance alone, a great coup, and that's all that's going on. It's a game, it's a chance operation, and people think they are doing something purposeful...but they're really not."

—MERTON MILLER, NOBEL LAUREATE, UNIVERSITY OF CHICAGO

"Contrary to their often articulated goal of outperforming the market averages, investment managers are not beating the market; the market is beating them."

—CHARLES D. ELLIS, *WINNING THE LOSER'S GAME*

CHAPTER 2

How Fees and Taxes Make Your Nest Egg Go Splat!

"The miracle of compounding returns is overwhelmed by the tyranny of compounding costs."

—JOHN BOGLE, FOUNDER OF THE VANGUARD GROUP

Wall Street might siphon away 33 percent of your money over ten to fifteen years if you let it. Sounds incredible, but the taxes and fees paid to Wall Street to beat the market will compound over time and can easily wipe out one third of your money. From 1925 to 2003, US stocks appreciated nearly 10.4 percent per year. Today, if you give Wall Street 2 percent in fees, you will lose an average of 20 percent of your investment profits. Add taxes to that, and you lose another 1 percent. That's 30 percent!

Then there are the unseen loses from unrealized compounding, and, with the help of active management, you'll give up more when the market does poorly. What should you do instead? Keep reading.

How to Keep Uncle Sam and Wall Street at Bay

(JULY 9, 2011)

You've got money to invest, but it seems that once you have a few bucks, everyone wants to put their hand in your pocket and keep it there—forever! We're not talking about your loser brother-in-law. We're talking about real business partners who want big percentages of all your returns.

Over the past eighty years, stocks have returned about 10 percent, while bonds have returned about 5 percent. An average balanced portfolio should therefore return around 7.5 percent over a long period. If you grow your money at 7.5 percent each year, you'll double your savings every nine to ten years. Let's call these *returns before advice and taxes.* This is the baseline.

Paying for investment help can be very expensive. If you pay mutual fund and advisory fees of 2.5 percent, you have a silent "business partner" who is taking a third of your 7.5 percent investment profits for advice. Over a twenty-year period, unless these advisers are making up the difference, which is statistically close to impossible, you lose big money—slowly, quietly, and imperceptibly. Your account will grow in good years, but it won't grow enough. Over time, you'll notice that everything is becoming more expensive and your portfolio is small, when years ago it seemed much larger.

INVESTING CAN BE TAXING

If investment advice doesn't do you in, taxes will. Mutual fund managers and advisers never report investment returns after tax because this would dramatically reduce returns. Most mutual fund managers are trading machines, generating huge amounts of short-term capital gains. But taxes are never factored into the advertising. Let's say that federal and state taxes are 40 percent on short-term gains and 20 percent on long-term gains. You invest in two funds. Let's call them the Furious Trading Fund and the Buy and Forget Fund. If Furious is up 15 percent, you'll net 10 percent after tax, but Buy and Forget only needs to be up 12.5 percent to net you same 10 percent after tax. Furious has to do 20 percent better than Buy and Forget to get you to the same place!

Smart investors don't pay much in taxes on their investments because they don't trade in and out of their positions. They spread their money around the world in different types of stocks and bonds based on their objectives (called asset allocation) using exchange-traded funds (ETFs). They own core portfolios, with most of their net worth consisting of ten to fifteen ETFs, to get nearly complete diversity in stocks, real estate, commodities, and bonds. Each ETF represents an entire stock or bond market that is an essential ingredient to a portfolio. They hold these same ETFs forever.

This is far from buying and holding. Over time, the relative proportions of each ETF within the portfolio will need to change. If bonds are up this year and stocks are down, it is critical to trim bond ETFs and to add to stock ETFs. As people age, they should start shifting more of their portfolio into bonds—same ETFs, different weightings.

Here's where taxes are minimized: after owning a passively managed ETF portfolio for one year, all gains from selling the ETFs are taxed at long-term rates. ETFs have a special tax structure that rarely generates taxable income except for dividends.

By trimming and adding, you only incur a small amount of long-term tax, but the gains continue to accrue tax-free. The smart investor tinkers around a few times a year, but never gets in and gets out.

If you keep Uncle Sam and Wall Street at bay, you can keep most of your returns. If you let them into your portfolio, you will find yourself half as rich as you could have been.

Who's Picking Your Pocket?

(FEBRUARY 27, 2010)

Years ago one of our daughters was pickpocketed in Manhattan while on an educational tour of the East Coast. In her ten-year-old mind, the shiny yellow zipper of her My Little Pony fanny pack provided all the protection she needed for her hard-earned spending money. Who would slip their grubby hands into an adorable little girl's fanny pack and rip her off in broad daylight? She received an education that day. She learned that such people exist, and that once you find out your money is gone, the thief is also long gone, enjoying the spoils of their plunder. The lesson? Keep a close eye on your money.

When it comes to retirement accounts, it behooves us to keep a close eye on who slips past our yellow-zippered firewalls to gain access to our hard-earned dollars. Although legal, mutual fund and wealth managers have a way of quietly dipping into our accounts through 12b-1 fees and other subtle techniques. Mercer Bullard, president and founder of Fund Democracy, a mutual fund shareholder advocacy organization, explained recently that 12b-1 fees are used to pay for a "grab bag of services" that help pump up mutual fund company profits.

Not all fees are bad, as long as we receive commensurate value. In a recent *Forbes* article, Rick Ferri explored how paying for active money management isn't worth the risk. You simply don't get what you pay for. David Berman recently reported on the annual Standard & Poor's actively managed scorecard for mutual funds. By merely going a short five years out, he found that just 7.45 percent of mutual funds beat the index.

So who's picking your pocket?

Warning! 50 Percent of Your Yearly IRA Contributions Goes to Fees

(APRIL 3, 2010)

In early spring 2010, individual retirement accounts (IRAs) came under the scrutiny of a variety of vigilant eyes, including CNN, a leading newspaper, and even the highest court in the land. The findings were shocking: the funds are raiding our nests at an alarming rate.

This week's news revealed a shockingly sad reality—50 percent of the annual $4,000 IRA contribution that most of us make goes to line the pockets of mutual fund managers. Detailed in the MarketRiders recent "Aggregate Mutual Fund Fee Report: US IRA Accounts 2009," our research showed how mutual fund fees can siphon away half of an individual's yearly contribution and, over many years, over a third of his or her total portfolio. CNN liked the report so much it did a segment on it last weekend. Even the Supreme Court weighed in with a highly anticipated decision concerning controversial mutual fund fees. The corruptive power of 12b-1 fees was also recently explored by the *Washington Post.*

It is hard to reject the powerful lure of mutual funds. That old Putnam money manager seems so convincing in those TV ads shown during the US Open or the Final Four. But mutual fund fees kill returns like cigarettes kill smokers. The evidence is overwhelming. By simply keeping fees down with indexed ETFs, globally diversifying, and rebalancing as the markets ebb and flow, we can escape the mutual fund con game and save 80 percent in fees. It may be boring, but every study indicates that you will end up retiring with a lot more money.

Five Ways to Keep Your Broker Honest

(DECEMBER 18, 2010)

Not everyone is a do-it-yourself investor. According to Forrester Research, 30 percent of all investors want to delegate their investment decisions to someone else. Unfortunately, most delegators will spend more time shopping for a car than calculating the true cost of the investment advice they use to protect their priceless nest eggs. If you are a delegator, here are some tips that will help minimize risk and give you a shot at having a successful relationship with your broker or investment manager.

1. Show me the fees. Most brokers are biased toward investing your money in mutual funds that kick back yearly marketing commissions—which you pay for. Our friend Scott had a $6-million account with one of the largest Wall Street firms and, to make our point, we calculated his mutual fund fees, loads, and extra costs. Last year he paid about $138,000! We switched his portfolio to a MarketRiders portfolio and now he pays $18,000 per year. The solution? Ask for a comprehensive list of all the fees you are paying annually, including those for each fund and your adviser's fees. Try to get these aggregate fees below 1.5 percent per year. To help get you started, we built a great mutual fund fee calculator.

2. Get invoiced. Most brokers take fees from your investment account through commissions and hidden charges. Registered investment advisers will often send you an invoice. Ask any adviser to send you an invoice, and write them a check. At a minimum, ask to be notified when fees are deducted. That way you'll stay aware of the cost for these services.

3. Show me the commissions. Ask your broker to disclose the exact amount of commissions, credits, and any form of compensation that will be received as an incentive for having you invest in a certain financial product such as a mutual fund, an annuity, or life insurance. Ask for the cost of an index fund alternative so that you can understand exactly what it is costing you to be sold a particular product. Equipped with this knowledge, you will be able to justify its price in the future.

4. Deduct taxes paid. The average turnover for a mutual fund is 70 percent a year. That means nearly all stocks in a portfolio are sold each year and traded for other stocks. Turnover can create taxable income at year-end. Each February, after these taxes are calculated, give your financial adviser your federal and state tax rates and ask him or her to add up the taxes generated by turnover in your funds. Then withdraw from your accounts the amount you need to pay the taxes, and you can figure out the true after-tax return. After all, that's what you keep.

5. Benchmarking. Many investors are happy when they make money in a fund, but that's how amateurs think. Endowment managers and elite institutions judge their financial advisers against a benchmark. Each manager must, net of fees, outperform a comparable index fund that charges far lower fees. Have your financial adviser pick a benchmark for each fund and measure the adviser's fund-picking skills by how well that fund performed versus its benchmark. For example, a friend was bragging last week about how well his small-cap fund was doing this year—it was up over 20 percent! We pointed out that the ETF we recommend in MarketRiders portfolios—iShares S&P Small Cap 600 Index (symbol IJR)—was up nearly 24 percent as of December 15. And that's just a computer-managed index of six hundred small-cap stocks picked by market capitalization. Our friend learned that he had paid 1.75 percent for underperformance, and the fund had 80 percent turnover this year, which was sure to create taxable income. IJR charges only 0.2 percent in fees and has rarely sent a tax bill to holders.

You worked hard for your money. These are reasonable ways to hold your broker accountable. Don't blame your broker if, in fifteen years, a good chunk of your retirement nest egg has been siphoned away in fees. He was just doing his job.

Is Your Broker Your Candy Man?

(JULY 10, 2010)

For some, "The Candy Man" is a fun ditty from the 1971 movie *Willie Wonka & the Chocolate Factory*, but the phrase has a much more sinister past. As stated in a May 1976 article in the *Oxford Journal*, the etymological origins of the term *candy man* are rooted in a historic coal miners' strike in 1863 England. The mining companies of the day hired itinerant confectionary salesmen to help evict striking miners from company-supplied housing. The phrase *candy man* soon became a derogatory term for someone who appears to be harmless and kind but has unperceived bad intent.

The revolution of the 1960s brought new meaning to the word. The candy man became a conniving drug pusher who offered unaware teens a good time through free or low-cost drugs. His strategic marketing plan was simple and has survived to this day—get kids hooked now and garner huge profits later.

Sadly, many brokers have taken a page out of the candy man's playbook. The promise of sagacious advice that will enhance one's wealth, provide access to elite and high-performing investment products, and deliver eye-popping performance statistics ridden with fine-print qualifiers lure in the investor. Quietly, the needle is slipped into the investor's brokerage account, and hard-to-detect commissions management, 12b-1, trading, and front-end and back-end fees drain away hard-earned savings. Wall Street reaps huge rewards while investors quietly lose.

Discharging a candy-man broker is often a scary proposition, but as many of our members have found, liberation from high-priced investment help is good for the spirit—and for the retirement account.

Should You Fire Your Broker?

(APRIL 9, 2011)

Burton Malkiel's famous tome *The Random Walk Guide to Investing* begins with the right exhortation for most investors: fire your broker today. Although it takes moxie to say no to that special someone who has earned your trust, the facts reveal that your investments will do far better without your wealth manager's hands dipping into your cookie jar.

The facts are plain to understand. According to the US Securities and Exchange Commission (SEC), the average broker charges 1.11 percent in annual fees to manage your money. This same broker is likely to put you into a portfolio of actively managed mutual funds that average more than 1 percent in fees.

That places a more than 2 percent burden on your portfolio and drags down performance.

Some investors think 2 percent is a small price to pay for expert guidance. What many fail to realize is that 2 percent represents a shocking 25-percent business partner in your annual earnings. With the average diversified portfolio earning around 8 percent annually, you are paying twenty-five cents on every dollar for "expert" help.

It is not uncommon for a business partner to invest large sums of money or to work for years to gain 25 percent ownership of a business. What is it that an investment adviser does that should result in such a favorable perch?

MYTHS ABOUT BROKERS

What about performance? Charles Ellis and other academics exposed active management as a loser's game decades ago. If that is hard for you to accept, add in adviser fees and it should be easy to see that your portfolio is doomed to underperform.

What about trust? Brokers sell many products, with trust being at the top of the list. How much can you trust a person who is willing to sell you high-fee, actively managed funds? Trust is an emotion that a smart investor should not heed. Strategy is key. If the broker fervently recommends indexing, then you have the first building block of trust.

What about allocations? How difficult is it in today's information age to obtain sophisticated asset allocations designed for your needs? Not hard at all. At MarketRiders, you can obtain a globally diversified allocation customized to your needs and optimized for your broker. There is no need to pay high fees for such guidance.

What about personal attention? The average broker or investment adviser has more than one hundred clients and is rewarded for new business development, not for taking a deep interest in current customers. Think about how difficult it must be to stay current on the specific needs of a client when you have ninety-nine others to think about and five more this week you are trying to close. Where do you think that adviser will put his energy? Toward new business and new revenue. Think about it. When was the last time your adviser contacted you?

REASONS TO KEEP YOUR BROKER

To problem solve. If you are faced with a unique set of problems, tax concerns, or major life decisions, hiring an expert may be a good decision to help you get on the right track. For problem solving, it is best to hire a financial planner who works by the hour. Get your problems solved and then move on.

Your "busyness." You may be so busy with your career and family responsibilities that the extra burden of managing your portfolio feels unbearable. Before you go with an adviser, be aware that managing a globally diversified indexed portfolio should take no more than a few hours a year. Even still, some may find the burden too heavy and want someone else to make the call. An adviser might be right for you.

To hold your hand. The most notable reason to have an investment adviser manage your accounts is for behavioral reasons. Research reveals that some investors have difficulty staying the course. Buying when the market is up and selling when it is down can be costly. Whipsawed by emotion and market hysteria, such investors would do far better having an adviser to oversee the disciplines of smart index investing. While such oversight will cost, being suckered in to the next stock tip, chasing trends, and timing the market will result in much greater damage than advisory fees ever could.

If you do hire an adviser, be sure they are committed to indexing, have reasonable flat-rate fees no greater than .75 percent of assets under management, and have transparent reporting and timely communication. Better yet, hand over a pink slip and take control of your own retirement. Either way, index, stay the course, and retire on schedule.

Experts Speak

"Memo to those who think it's okay to pay fees of 3 percent or more... those fees will eat up most—or all—of your future gains. The fees may look small, relative to the investment earnings you expect. But that's because you overestimate what the market actually yields."

—JANE BRYANT QUINN, AUTHOR

"Investment fees of all sorts may well amount to 20 percent of the earnings of American business. The burden of paying investment managers may cause equity investors to earn only 80 percent of what they would earn if they just sat still and listened to no one."

—WARREN BUFFETT, BERKSHIRE HATHAWAY

"Properly measured, the average actively managed dollar must underperform the average passively managed dollar, net of costs. Empirical analyses that appear to refute this principle are guilty of improper measurement."

—WILLIAM F. SHARPE, NOBEL LAUREATE, STANFORD UNIVERSITY

"Most investors, both institutional and individual, will find the best way to own common stocks is through an index fund that charges minimal fees. Those following this path are sure to beat the net results (after fees and expenses) delivered by the great majority of investment professionals."

—WARREN BUFFETT, BERKSHIRE HATHAWAY

CHAPTER 3

The Calculus of Trust

"There are two kinds of investors: those who don't know where the market is headed, and those who don't know that they don't know. Then again, there is a third type of investor—the investment professional, who indeed knows that he or she doesn't know, but whose livelihood depends upon appearing to know."

—DR. WILLIAM BERNSTEIN, AUTHOR

If you think brokers, mutual fund managers, and many investment advisers are looking out for you, check your back. There's an inherent conflict at play here. You're looking for a risk–return ratio that increases your investment value. They're looking to increase their own income through commissions, fees, and needless activity. We want to make money. They want to take money. In this chapter, you will learn about different types of advisers, how they charge, what motivates them, and how to work with them—if you dare. It's a revealing look at a subject that flies under most people's radar—but not ours.

What Makes You Trust Anyone's Investment Advice?

(SEPTEMBER 30, 2011)

It is well documented in surveys and studies by financial institutions that when we seek investment help, we make choices based on one major criterion: trust. It all boils down to this one word. Who is giving the advice? Can I trust them?

If you are a hard-core, do-it-yourself investor who loves to day trade, you may trust the Motley Fool or the Daily Options Trader based on the success of their recommendations. If you delegate your investing, you may trust your friend's son who works at Smith Barney. You know, the one who got his MBA at Wharton and plays with your kids.

Con men and Ponzi scheme operators know how to get our trust by playing with our fears and our greed. The SEC knows it can't regulate trust, but it does regulate how advisers engender it. Thanks to laws from the 1930s, an investment adviser cannot advertise testimonials from other clients. That's why you never see advertisements showing celebrities like Oprah crowing, "Joe Morningstar is my favorite money manager! He helped me buy this estate in Maui!" In fact, social networks cause panic for many investment advisers today. We wonder: if a client "likes" an adviser on Facebook, is he endorsing the service and leaving the adviser open to an SEC investigation?

We may look at the past performance of mutual funds to gauge our level of trust, but this has been proven fallacious at best (thus the fine print noting that "past performance is no indication of future results"). As we've written many times, the game of performance reporting is rigged. A bad mutual fund can buy up a high-performing one and assume the latter's track record.

But when it gets down to it, we must trust someone or something before handing over our dough. Unfortunately, most investors fly blindly without ever thinking through the question of who should earn their trust and why. We continually encounter investors who own a variety of mutual funds, pay enormous fees, and have no idea that they are engaged in active investing. They believe that if they are buying products from a large institution, then they'll achieve their goals. We meet investors who have delegated managing their money to an individual because he was on *Barron's* Top Financial Advisers list. Others find status by being able to say, "I'm a Goldman client."

Giving trust is a complex emotional dynamic that we'll leave to the shrinks to articulate. What can we learn about trust from the smartest investors in the world? Do the trustees of Yale sit with prospective hedge fund managers, look them in the eye, and then have a discussion about who has better eye contact and a more confident handshake? No. They develop investment trust not by emotions or instincts, but through a logical evaluation of three dimensions, in the following order.

THE PROCESS

First and foremost, smart investors invest with an investment methodology. They adhere to a philosophical approach that they believe to be true about investing. For instance, Warren Buffett fans believe in buying out-of-favor, inefficiently priced stocks and holding them until everyone else changes their opinion. At MarketRiders, we focus on finding the right asset allocation and then recommending low-cost ETFs and a consistent rebalancing protocol. Vanguard fund owners have generally bought into the idea that low fees will make them more money, so they like passive investing instead of active investing. Whether or not you know anything about investing, you need to spend some time learning about the various investing "religions" and developing your own point of view.

THE INSTITUTION

Institutions come and go, as we've seen with Lehman Brothers and Bear Stearns. A "Wall Street legacy" is an oxymoron. The names come and go. But doing business with a firm with a culture and track record of delivering on your process is nonetheless vitally important. The firm needs to be solid and have checks and balances and high standards of compliance. Why does Vanguard have over a trillion dollars under management? Because Jack Bogle's original vision to help working Americans by building a not-for-profit organization has remained intact. Vanguard continually lowers its fees as it adds assets, and it adheres to its process of passive investing.

THE PERSON

If you have a belief in an investment process and have found an institution that embraces that process, then trusting the individual with whom you work becomes the last piece of the equation. Make sure regulators have not sanctioned the individual and ask for background information. This should be the last step, not the first, in establishing trust. Trusting people and institutions before you've first developed a core belief about investing gets the whole thing backward. Understand the various investment philosophies and develop your own point of view, and then look for people and institutions to help you implement it.

Why Your Broker Doesn't Put You First

(JUNE 24, 2011)

Have your heard the following old tale? During a flood, a kind-hearted frog lets a scorpion ride to safety on his back. Just as they reach the middle of the river, the scorpion stings the frog. As they both sink beneath the waves, the frog asks, "Why did you sting me?"

"It's my nature," the scorpion replies. "That's what I do."

When you choose someone to help you with financial advice, it is important to know "what they do." In professions where the provider is helping individuals in highly personal and important areas like health, credentials mean that the person has earned the right to be trusted. There are understood standards and norms. Doctors are credentialed in the field of medicine. Chiropractors have a different type of training than oncologists. We know who we are seeing and what they are supposed to be able to do. Attorneys who have passed the bar graduated from law school and have the legal right to practice.

Such clear certification is very confusing in financial services. It may seem as though a professional broker at Merrill Lynch or Morgan Stanley provides the same service as someone who is a registered investment adviser, but nothing could be further from the truth. This distinction is critical to understand no matter how much you trust the individual.

THE TRUTH ABOUT CREDENTIALS

A person who is a broker is just that. He acts as an agent between a buyer and seller of products, usually for a commission. Legally, those who work for a broker or dealer must pass a Series 7 exam, which teaches them about the stock market and securities to prepare them to sell commissioned products. Brokers operate by a suitability standard under which they are required to make investments they judge to be suitable for clients. A broker can't sell microcap volatile stocks to old ladies. Brokers and their firms are governed by a self-regulated organization (not a government agency) called FINRA. In the industry, brokers are measured by the amount of commissions and fees they generate from selling products. Product providers pay more for distribution through brokers.

Registered investment advisers (RIAs) help individuals manage their money. They must pass a Series 65 exam, which tests how well they know how to help a client invest and operate under a fiduciary standard. This means an adviser is required to act in his or her clients' best interests and disclose to them all conflicts of interest. These advisers are either registered in the state in which they operate or with the SEC. RIAs are usually measured by assets under management (AUM) because the more assets they manage, the greater their fee income. They submit lengthy ADV II forms online showing any conflicts of interest, sanctions from the SEC, and exactly how they are paid.

RIAs can't use customer testimonials in advertising and must disclose when they pay for client referrals. Brokers can use testimonials and hide fees they receive for referrals. Under Dodd-Frank, legislators are considering implementing a fiduciary standard for brokers—who are fit to be tied. The central issue is that if brokers are required to put your interests ahead of theirs, they will have to disclose conflicts of interest and fees.

FINRA is spending a fortune to fight the proposal because if brokers disclose all fees they receive, investors will get wise and FINRA members will earn less. FINRA's CEO earned nearly $3 million last year, and FINRA's top ten employees earned over $1 million each. FINRA doesn't want its members to pay them less, so everyone is pulling out all the stops.

BROKER VERSUS ADVISER: MANAGE OR ADVISE?

A good analogy for explaining the difference between a broker and an investment adviser is an optometrist and an ophthalmologist. An optometrist conducts eye exams and makes sure your eyes are healthy, but he or she primarily makes money selling glasses and contact lenses. When you have a more serious condition, such as cataracts, you go to a medical doctor—an ophthalmologist. She or he has taken the Hippocratic oath to practice medicine ethically. She sells nothing; she puts your health first.

Do you want to trust your money to someone who is paid just for advice? Or would you prefer a broker who makes money, providing advice in order to sell products?

Remember: if you're carrying someone across the river, you may want to know "what they do."

Hiring a Money Manager–Buyer Beware!

(MARCH 20, 2010)

We were discussing this week's news and feeling no pity for Bernie Madoff, who was roughed up in prison the other day. It reminded Steve about his first experience being scammed. It's a great story we wanted to share.

"It happened to me when I was a spry, wide-eyed fourteen-year-old. I had recently become fascinated with fine electric guitars, fostered by my occasional visits to the legendary Leo's Music in Berkeley, California. I would jump on my skateboard, slide my way down the Oakland Hills, and jump onto an AC Transit bus to make my way to the dimly lit wonderland of rock music—Leo's. With a constant flow of hard-core rockers and up-and-coming wannabes gliding through the doors, and the black walls lined with vintage guitars from Fender, Gibson, Rickenbacker, and more, Leo's was a portal into a dimension far different from my upper-middle-class home in the hills. Of all the instruments there, the crown jewel was the Gibson Les Paul Custom. My teenage mind could not comprehend how one instrument could cost $2,000 in 1974, but I knew I needed one.

"Weeks passed, and my desire for the guitar grew. Then by a strange twist of fate, my friend knew of a guy who had a Les Paul that he urgently needed to unload. I met the seller and thought it seemed too good to be true. I was holding a beautiful black Les Paul Custom in my hands—and it could be mine for a mere $150. I rushed home and gave my father the most compelling sales pitch of my life: Leo's pricing, man in need, played it myself, collection for my paper route in one week, can gladly pay next Tuesday for a hamburger today, and so on. My father suspected a lesson was at hand and forwarded me the cash with a warning I will never forget. He said, 'Caveat emptor. Let the buyer beware.'

"I rushed back, made the purchase, and zipped home to my dad like a proud dog with a bone. I carefully handed the guitar to him with great pride. He took one look at it and said, 'Hmm, this is interesting. Do you see this here?' There it was, in very small print hidden under the neck: Made in China. The scammer had taken a cheap replica and replaced all the badges with authentic Les Paul hardware."

Every few weeks we are reminded that the investment world scams smart people. With a globally diversified MarketRiders ETF portfolio, there's no need to carefully look "under the neck" of each investment we make. Instead of owning a few stocks, you can own thousands. Instead of having a crooked fund manager, you can own an index. You can waltz by the scammers and invest with peace of mind.

Who Is on Your Side?

(APRIL 17, 2010)

Financial scandals made headlines in 2010 as Goldman Sachs was investigated for securities violations. ETFs were looking better and better as safe havens for investing.

Just when we thought we were through hearing about the Wall Street hooligans and their criminal vices, our "untouchable" friends at Goldman Sachs made the news twice. The *Wall Street Journal* revealed that the SEC had found criminal doings at Goldman. One hand was secretly cramming worthless mortgage-backed securities into their valued clients' accounts, while the other was placing big bets against that very same market. And if that wasn't enough, one of Goldman's directors was implicated as part of the Galleon hedge fund insider trading racket—the biggest ever in America. Goldman Sachs's slogan, "Helping clients build and preserve their financial wealth," needs a minor adjustment: "Helping clients build and preserve *our* financial wealth."

When it comes to retirement investing, you don't have as many friends in the financial services industry as you think. By taking the time to learn the virtues of low-cost indexing, global diversification, and disciplined rebalancing, you will truly build and preserve your wealth.

Do You Want Assets Under–or Out of–Management?

(JUNE 26, 2010)

The Gulf Oil Disaster brought ashore a concept that can poison our faith in humanity. To some people, the little guy really doesn't count.

A few weeks ago British Petroleum (BP) CEO Tony Hayward felt the heat of America's ire for his "I want my life back" gaffe. This week, BP Chairman Carl-Henric Svanberg may have outdone him, commenting before Congress that "BP cares about the small people." After eleven deaths, destruction of Gulf fisheries, and a local economy in shambles, his reference to the "small people" landed on sensitive nerves.

Whether a simple language blunder or insight into the psychology of the rich and powerful, Svanberg's comments touched on a belief held by many—that in this world there are rules for the privileged and separate rules for the rest of us, conjuring up memories of the late Leona Helmsley's famous statement that "only the little people pay taxes."

LITTLE PEOPLE VERSUS BIG PEOPLE

Wall Street was founded on the little people premise. One manifestation of it can be understood from the ubiquitous conversation had by wealth managers about assets under management (AUM). AUM is the measuring rod of their success and compensation, which is a topic of their urbane, cocktail-party banter. Every wealth manager or investment adviser is aware of his own AUM as well as that of his or her friends and competitors because it indicates how much one earns.

Wealth managers trim 1 percent to 1.5 percent in fees from "their" AUM every year. The bigger your retirement account, the more you add to your manager's AUM, and the bigger you become in his or her eyes. If your account is under $500,000, you are likely a little person. Some top managers won't answer your phone calls if you can't add $5 million to their AUM.

At MarketRiders, we've begun measuring our success, in part, by Assets Out of Management (AOM). We track the amount of draining fees from the AUM game that we've helped you escape. This week, we celebrated reaching $500 million in AOM, and thousands of investors are now saving millions in fees and investing with less risk. Here's to no little people!

Trust and Hidden Agendas

(AUGUST 28, 2010)

The best-selling book *Freakonomics* chronicles the search for the hidden incentives behind all sorts of behavior. It characterizes the field of economics as the study of incentives: how people get what they want or need, especially when other people want or need the same thing. *Freakonomics* gives entertaining examples of how odd results can be explained by carefully evaluating people's incentives, such as how cheating can be applied to teachers and sumo wrestlers, and why most crack cocaine dealers are willing to live in near-poverty conditions.

There is no industry more ridden with conflicts of interest and misaligned incentives than investment management. David Swensen, chief investment officer at Yale University (one of our MarketRiders experts), writes, "Relationships with external investment managers provide a fertile breeding ground for conflicts of interests…[We] seek high risk-adjusted returns, while outside investment advisers pursue substantial, stable flows of fee income."

UNDERSTANDING INCENTIVES

To properly evaluate any financial advice, you must understand the incentives of the adviser. If your broker or insurance agent is your best friend, remember that he feeds his family by selling you products that may not be best for you. The financial adviser you pay by the hour may talk a little too much and be pedantic in delivering his advice to keep the meter running. Those who are paid a percentage of your assets want more of your money.

A HIGHER STANDARD

Regulations in the financial services industry put another and more subtle dimension on incentives for advisers. Did you know that a broker/dealer works under different legal standards than a registered investment adviser? Did you know that a certified financial planner must pass much more rigorous examinations than brokers or advisers?

Speaking of incentives, our August 14 newsletter comparing the mutual fund industry to the tobacco industry ended up in the *New York Times,* which prompted the vice president of research at Morningstar to make dismissive comments about our arguments. Applying the *Freakonomics* concept, we publicly bet him that a portfolio of ten ETFs recommended by MarketRiders would beat ten five-star-rated Morningstar mutual funds. He refused to accept our wager. We weren't at all surprised. After all, he'll make much more money perpetuating the myth that his system works than losing his own money by actually using it.

Burned Notice: Wall Street's Hidden Perils

(OCTOBER 2, 2010)

During his summer break from college, my son tried to sell me on the merits of the popular TV series *Burn Notice*. In this drama, Jeffrey Donovan plays Michael Westen, a former covert operative who unjustly receives a "burn notice"—an espionage-style termination that results in the immediate eradication of his assets and influence, leaving him isolated and alone.

The finance industry has a similar practice. I call it the "burned notice." The courts call it a Notice of Pendency of Class Actions. Ironically, within days of my son's eloquent appeal for the TV show, I received another one of many burned notices, this one from the United States District Court of Maryland. This notice came courtesy of the fine work of Strong Mutual Funds and my former investment advisers.

Somehow, the folks at Strong had found a way to accidentally commit the crimes of market timing, short-term or excessive trading, and various forms of portfolio churning—all of which resulted in a $140 million settlement for 458 thousand burned investors. The burned notice instructed me that I should simply and carefully read pages of legalese, research my past holdings (which, by the way, I never knew I had courtesy of my former wealth manager's fund-of-funds investment methodology), enter the correct data (better not miss a detail), and mail the document to receive some unknown amount from the settlement. How does that sound as a pleasant way to spend your Saturday afternoon?

HIDDEN RISK

My mutual fund journey painfully reminded me of the important concept of agency risk: the possibility that a firm's manager will not act in the best interest of its shareholders. With each intermediary between you and your hard-earned retirement dollars, you compound agency risk. Introduce an investment advisory? Agency risk. Buy mutual funds? Agency risk. Have your investment adviser place your money into a fund-of-funds? Agency risk upon agency risk.

It was not that long ago that most of us lived with a prevailing sense of cosmic responsibility. Agency risk was not a common topic of conversation. Those were the days when most fiduciaries believed they should do the right thing—even when no one was looking.

Today, the Wall Street ethos has sadly crept further toward a get-rich-at-others'-expense mentality. From the macabre and guiltless grin of Bernie Madoff to the quiet SEC payoff this month by Goldman Sachs and the brazen collateralized debt obligations hoisted upon the public's shoulders, investors have become wise to the fact that Wall Street can no longer be implicitly trusted to work in their best interests.

ETHICS INTO EXTINCTION

As much as I want to like the fat old gray-haired guy in the Smith Barney commercial who espouses—with a British accent to boot—that the company makes money the old-fashioned way, I'm wise to shirk the rhetoric in favor of the facts. The old-fashioned way is long gone for many money managers. I alone must keep a keen eye on my retirement dollars. There are few I can trust to do it for me and even fewer I can trust to do it well.

Removing agency risk eliminates a very real threat to preserving your hard-earned retirement wealth and delivers peace of mind. By managing a diversified portfolio of low-cost, exchange-traded funds, you can sleep peacefully at night knowing that a Madoff is not is not lurking somewhere in your portfolio.

Meanwhile, the mutual fund crowd is saddled with the burden of wondering if their burned notices are coming in the mail.

Is Your Money Safe With Your Broker?

(MAY 13, 2011)

In the wake of brokerage scandals, banks gone bust, and funds gone AWOL, investors faced new fears that trickled down to the safety of their money. "Do no harm" was clearly not the mantra of a sick financial industry.

When Lehman Brothers went bankrupt in September 2008, most investors faced a question they had never considered: is my money safe with my broker? What happened to Lehman's brokerage accounts, and what makes one broker, like Fidelity, safer than another?

To get to the bottom of this question, we caught up with Michael Hogan, CEO of FOLIOfn Investments Inc. When stock markets began, brokers physically traded share certificates of a company's stock, and armed guards moved certificates between brokers and their vaults all day long. In the 1960s there was a back-office crisis as trading volume went from 5 million shares daily to 15 million shares. The paperwork burden was overwhelming, and brokers and stock exchanges came together to form the Depository Trust and Clearing Corporation (DTC).

Fast forward to our highly automated world. Today there are no share certificates—only records of how many shares are owned and by whom. The DTC is the heart of the system and tracks the shares of all securities held by all brokers. When the trading is over, the brokers settle between one another through the DTC. IBM stock held in a Schwab brokerage account is held in Schwab's name, or "street name," at the DTC. If you sell one hundred shares of IBM to someone at Merrill Lynch, that night the DTC will transfer shares from Merrill to Schwab and cash from Schwab to Merrill. Schwab keeps track of which clients own how many shares. The DTC acts like a huge backup system for stocks, bonds, and cash in brokerage accounts.

WHO HOLDS THE MONEY?

Anyone can pass a test and become a broker, but *clearing* brokers are part of the elite group plugged directly into the DTC system. There are hundreds of clearing brokers and thousands of introducing brokers. All introducing brokers must clear through a clearing broker.

Clearing brokers hold money and securities and need multimillion-dollar IT infrastructures to process orders and to keep accounts and the capital to deliver securities or pay for them. "The bar is high," Hogan says. "Clearing brokers must demonstrate to regulators that they have the capability to be part of this highly regulated system. They must reconcile cash and securities on a nearly daily basis with the DTC and all other firms, and are audited every week."

The Securities Investor Protection Corporation (SIPC) restores cash and securities to investors with assets in the hands of bankrupt or otherwise financially troubled brokerage firms. SIPC provides up to $500,000 of protection for brokerage accounts and estimates that no fewer than 99 percent of people who are eligible have been made whole in the failed brokerage cases it has handled.

Brokers go broke because of bad management or fraud. Lehman went bankrupt because of bad management. SIPC and the DTC quickly restored investor accounts with another broker. As long as the records of the brokerage firm are accurate, and no other fraud was involved, investors get their securities and cash returned to them or moved to another broker within a month or two.

BE CLEAR ABOUT TYPES OF BROKERS

When fraud is involved, it is generally at the level introducing brokers, who are able to cash checks and create fake books. It is nearly impossible for clearing brokers to commit fraud. Hogan says, "The main way the system breaks down is when you deal with an introducing broker, and you're told to deposit money with their firm. They steal it and circumvent the system and create statements with a color printer. You're disconnected from reality and don't have a cross-check."

Hogan offers two pieces of advice if you don't use a clearing broker. When using introducing brokers, only make out your check to the clearing broker, and get access to the clearing broker's website so you can see your account. While introducing brokers have their own branded websites and statements, you should have online access to the clearing broker. Check your balances frequently. In addition, make sure regulators have never sanctioned your broker.

As long as you keep your securities and cash with a clearing brokerage that has been around for at least ten years and is run by competent management with a strong financial statement and an unblemished regulatory record, your money is safe.

Three Investment Lessons from the Fall of the Insider King

(MAY 20, 2011)

In spring 2011, a hedge fund guru's empire imploded and a nefarious network of insider trading was revealed. It was another example of how trusted advisers can deceive their clients.

Raj Rajaratnam, founder of the Galleon Group Hedge Fund, was found guilty this past Wednesday in what has become the new high-water mark for insider trading convictions. Lining his pockets with over $63.8 million in illegal windfall from his insider scam, this once-humble Sri Lankan son of a sewing machine company manager grew in physical, egotistical, and financial stature. Through swollen cheeks he crowed to friends about his $7-billion hedge fund empire, stating that the name Raj, which stands for *king* in Sri Lankan, makes him the "king of kings." How about the Insider King instead?

Indeed, Raj Rajaratnam gorged himself like a king, but on more than just Kobe beef. Using techniques once reserved for organized crime, drug trafficking, and terror plots, the Justice Department was able to convict the Insider King of nineteen counts of security-related fraud. His conviction involved a complex web of over twenty-three known complicit parties, ranging from corporate executives to hedge fund managers, revealing just how deep the insider culture runs among the Wall Street elite.

With the spotlight temporarily on this aspect of the malevolent hedge fund underworld, it behooves us to underscore a few key lessons for the everyday investor.

LESSON #1: THE LITTLE GUY CAN'T WIN ON WALL STREET

Every now and again you run into a day trader or active investor who has discovered the "golden cross" of technical analysis or has gained some yet-to-be perceived insight into the global economy that he is poised to exploit.

Forget the fact that thousands of financial researchers churned out of the top Ivy League schools are employed by leading hedge funds and are equipped with staggering research budgets, sophisticated analysis technologies, and shocking financial rewards for success.

Forget that these researchers are probably a bit smarter than you. Forget that they crunch data on autopilot, day after day, looking for an edge. Forget that even if the playing field were level, you would have to be a bit deluded to want to compete against such formidable opponents. Then add to that the simple, Insider King–illustrated reality that these organizations sometimes get trading information first—illegally—and the answer becomes simple. The little guy cannot win.

For the individual investor, active stock trading is like Popeye fighting Bluto—with no spinach in sight. Such a contest is so one-sided that it goes beyond entertaining to pathetic and downright disgusting. As the Las Vegas adage goes, look around the poker table, and if you can't spot the sucker, it's you.

LESSON #2: FEES REALLY MATTER

What does two and twenty mean to you? Probably not much, unless you've read the prospectus for a hedge fund. The going rate for playing the hedge fund game is a 2 percent annual management fee on assets under management plus a 20 percent profit share on all earnings. This is the fee burden the hedge fund manager must overcome to return value to the investor group.

With such a heavy fee burden, how do long-short equity hedge fund managers return value? They do it by building teams that perform deep research and astute analysis and use rapid response systems that exploit even the smallest window of opportunity. And sometimes they do it with the use of insider information, as the Insider King showed us. Surprisingly, even with all these resources and advantages, many hedge funds fail to beat the market over time. Two and twenty is a lot to overcome.

LESSON #3: SOME THINGS NEVER CHANGE

Yes, the Galleon verdict is an encouraging example of justice, but just how deep is the insider problem? According to the Cayman Islands Monetary Authority, there are over five thousand hedge funds representing more than $2.3 trillion in investments. And although many of these funds conduct ethical enterprises, the dollars at play provide a substantial motive for misbehavior. Galleon is just the tip of the iceberg.

When malfeasance is involved, however, investors are frustrated by the fact that many cases are lost in court or end with nothing more than a wrist slap. The not-guilty verdicts awarded to Bear Stearns hedge-fund managers accused of misleading clients, Angelo Mozilo's multimillion-dollar settlement to erase fraud charges with the SEC, and the lack of indictments against Wall Street executives for misdeeds in the financial crisis are all examples of injustice. One commentator likened these efforts to a fruitless and frenetic game of whack-a-mole. You may strike a mole here and there, but a lot more disappear into their holes without facing consequences for their actions.

Although we applaud the conviction of the Insider King, when it comes to Wall Street, some things never change.

The individual investor need not despair. Through simple indexing and global diversification, you can tap into the value of corporate productivity and global economic growth and thereby sidestep the rigged world of active trading. Add to this the discipline of vigilantly driving down all unnecessary fees within your portfolio, and, in the end, you may have the last laugh.

The Trust Conundrum: A Way Out

(FEBRUARY 13, 2010)

This week *Wall Street Journal* writer Jason Zweig reported that investor Philip Eberlin allegedly put 80 percent of his assets in certificates of deposit and fixed annuities because "I don't have trust in Wall Street to help the small investor in any way, shape, or form."

Who or what is this evil beast called Wall Street? When we blame it for all financial woes, what exactly are we blaming?

Goldman Sachs? Warren Buffett (he owns a lot of Goldman)? Is Wall Street your life insurance company, the credit card companies, your mutual funds, your brokers, the banks, or the investment banks?

The fact is that none of us are sure, but it doesn't matter because we don't have much power over this ominous Wall Street anyway, whatever it is. But it's clear that a Wall Street does exist that we, as individuals, can prevent from damaging us.

WHAT WALL STREET WANTS

Most financial institutions want to control our money, which in turn gives them a unique opportunity to bill us for fees that we don't see or don't understand. Because we're not writing checks for these fees, we tend not to pay attention as our money flows from our pockets into theirs. That's where the trouble starts!

Put $25,000 into a mutual fund and you're hiring a Wall Street stock picker and paying him around $400 per year. He and his fund now control your money. Hire a financial adviser or a broker to manage your account, and there you go again! Wall Street controls your money.

Here's where Mr. Eberlin has it wrong, though. If I buy an ETF of fifteen hundred US companies, I own a part of all of them: IBM, Coca Cola, Disney, and Microsoft. There's no Wall Street. A broker may hold my security, but I am not being charged to invest. I own great businesses, and my distrust of Wall Street is not a factor.

When you buy low-cost ETFs according to a prudent asset allocation, you take Wall Street's hand out of your pocket. You're in control of your own money.

John Spence documented the seismic changes that must happen to encourage investors to wake up and yank Wall Street out of their pockets. Brokers like Schwab and Fidelity have announced new plans that give investors huge incentives to sell their mutual funds and buy all-ETF portfolios. Responsible journalists such as John Waggoner of *USA Today* are helping investors learn which ETFs to stay away from.

In the coming years, trends like these will reduce Wall Street's fees, which will weaken its grip over Americans and their money. We hope you're riding these trends with us.

Experts Speak

"It is amazing how difficult it is for a man to understand something when he is paid a small fortune to not understand it."

—JOHN BOGLE, FOUNDER OF THE VANGUARD GROUP

"Santa Claus and the Easter Bunny should take a few pointers from the mutual-fund industry. All three are trying to pull off elaborate hoaxes. But while Santa and the bunny suffer the derision of eight-year-olds everywhere, actively-managed stock funds still have an ardent following among otherwise clear-thinking adults."

—JONATHAN CLEMENTS, *WALL STREET JOURNAL*

"One must conclude that in general a manager's fee, and not his skill, plays the biggest role in performance. The higher the fee, the lower the performance."

—EUGENE FAMA, NOBEL LAUREATE, UNIVERSITY OF CHICAGO

PART TWO

How to Protect Your Pocket

CHAPTER 4

Spreading Your Money, Feeling The Joy

"Asset allocation is the foundation upon which portfolios should be constructed and managed."

—CHARLES D. ELLIS, AUTHOR OF *WINNING THE LOSER'S GAME*

Have you ever been at a cocktail party where the conversation turned to the markets and investing? It doesn't take long before someone mentions their good fortune of having invested in Apple in 2009 when it was eighty-two dollars a share. That story is usually met by yet a better tale detailing how one fortunate investor bought Google shares at eighty dollars, only to see them soar to over $600. The oohs and aahs are palpable—and the stories are true!

Who in their right mind would want to park their money in a slow-moving index fund when such rewards await the astute investor? Unfortunately, as we learned in Chapter 1 when we discussed active versus passive management, stock picking is an art akin to throwing darts at the stock page in the newspaper.

When you examine the investment behavior of the truly wealthy, you can learn a lot about what the best minds money do to preserve and grow wealth. We're not talking about the millionaire next door, but the billionaire a few towns or even a few states over, and the many multibillion-dollar endowments managed by elite institutions such as Yale, Harvard, and beyond. The super rich do not focus their energies on CNBC, Jim Cramer, or the next bit stock tip, but on scientifically determining an optimal global asset allocation across a myriad of asset classes. They do this for a simple and scientifically proven reason—because, over time, 90 percent of all returns come from asset allocation, not stock picking.

We began MarketRiders and wrote this book to bring the methodology used by the truly wealthy to ordinary investors like you. Although Wall Street keeps this low-fee approach hidden, you can follow its fundamental asset allocation practices by observing the advice supplied in these pages.

What the Heck Is Asset Allocation?

(APRIL 2, 2011)

Yale professors studied money managers to uncover the source of their portfolio performance and found that 90 percent of the returns came from the markets they invested in. Less than 10 percent came from individual stocks or was the result of timing. For example, if they owned small-cap value stocks and that group of stocks did well in a given year, the performance of that market was the source of their success, not the specific small-cap stocks they had chosen.

That's why sophisticated investors focus heavily on setting well-defined targets for how they allocate assets. To be an asset allocator, you must play by different rules. Every portfolio needs six or seven core asset classes. Conventional wisdom says you should have at least 5 percent of your portfolio—but no more than 30 percent—in a core asset class.

We provide allocations from the following core asset classes in all MarketRiders portfolios:

- US stocks
- International stocks
- Emerging Market stocks
- Bonds
- TIPS (Treasury Inflation Protected) bonds
- Real Estate
- Commodities

How is a core asset class defined? It has three primary characteristics:

A UNIQUE PURPOSE

Like each instrument in a jazz band, each asset class plays a valuable role in different economic circumstances. US Treasury bonds protect against economic meltdowns like the one experienced in 2008, but they lose value from inflation and slow down overall portfolio growth. Real estate hedges against inflation, provides a steady income stream, and can appreciate like stocks, but it is not immune to economic cycles.

Stocks have outperformed every other asset class since 1928, but, as we've seen, they can become overvalued and suffer a decade of volatility and mediocre performance. If the United States is growing slowly and countries such as India and China are outperforming, investing in foreign stocks gives you a hedge.

MARKET-BASED RETURNS

Core asset classes generate returns from a market, not the skill of an investment manager. For example, venture capital, private equity, and hedge funds derive their returns based on who the manager is and how accomplished he or she is—not from actual skill. As such, these are not core asset classes.

ACCESS

While many consider fine art to be an asset class, most everyday investors can't build a diversified portfolio of paintings, coins, and antiques. The asset class must be broad and deep enough to invest in. It must have a well-established marketplace not made up of trendy concoctions promoted by Wall Street financial engineers. Managed futures are not considered an asset class.

Non-core asset classes satisfy two of the three characteristics above. Examples would be venture capital, private equity, and hedge funds. Endowment managers and wealthy families have the resources and expertise to build portfolios consisting of 20 percent to 25 percent venture, hedge, or private equity funds, but most of us can't do this. Some investors are sold on using a fund of funds to invest in these asset classes but never consider such issues as whether they can trust the sponsor or whether the sponsor has conflicts of interest embedded in the fee structures. Moving to the art of asset allocation shows how this gets tricky. A few examples follow.

ALLOCATION STRATEGIES

When you become an asset allocator, you start thinking about issues like these:

SECTORS

There are ten basic economic sectors, and within each are industries. Communications equipment and software are industries within the technology sector. Sectors are not asset classes, with the exception of the real estate sector, which is a core asset class. The US real estate sector includes apartment buildings, warehouses, office buildings, and retail malls. It tends to behave differently from the overall US economy. Your house is not an allocation to real estate because its returns are mostly psychological and are limited to residential real estate in your town.

STYLES

For thirty years, a great allocation strategy has been to parse out small public companies that have a value bent and allocate to small-cap value stocks. This has added significant returns to portfolios.

COMMODITIES

In the past five years, allocating to commodities has become more acceptable for portfolios, but the debate rages on regarding how to allocate among gold, precious metals, energy, and agricultural products.

Start thinking about your portfolio through an asset-allocation lens. You'll start wondering what you have and how it will work in the next market rise or meltdown. Now we're talking!

Does Your Portfolio Have the Help of an Entire Peloton?

(AUGUST 7, 2010)

A peloton is a large group of bicyclists that move together in a pack. At MarketRiders, we sometimes describe asset allocation like the peloton in the Tour de France. In the front, a strong rider *pulls*—a term for breaking the wind for the rest of the group. The lead rider must work up to 25 percent harder to help the peloton while the other riders enjoy drafting behind this lead rider. Once the lead rider becomes exhausted, he pulls back into the group, letting the next rider move forward to take the pull. Cyclists call this "pace lining," and they know that by working together, they will, over the length of the race, achieve a significantly higher speed than riding alone. Even Lance Armstrong in his heyday could not come close to holding an individual pace that could match the speed produced through the shared work of the peloton.

Asset classes behave similarly. For a season, one asset class will be out front, outperforming. Sure enough, in time that asset class tires and drops back. Another asset class moves forward to pull your portfolio closer to your retirement goal. By keeping your target exposure intact in all your asset classes through disciplined rebalancing, you benefit the same way a cyclist does in the peloton, always enjoying the work of a strong asset class that is leading your portfolio forward.

A SHOCKING FACT

Asset allocation—spreading one's money into different buckets or asset classes—accounts for 90 percent of a portfolio's return over time. This leaves a paltry 10 percent of performance tied to security selection and market timing.

When you turn on CNBC or tune into Jim Cramer, you don't hear cogent discussion on asset allocation. Rather, you hear an expert waxing eloquent about his current prognostications on the market's direction or which stock to buy or sell—market timing and stock selection advice. As the finance media spins like a whirling dervish over these matters, many investors wring their hands and wonder if they should buy or sell, get in or get out. All the while, real returns are being determined by the investor's ability to identify and rebalance to asset allocations.

Asset allocation worked just like pace lining over the past ten years—a period billed as the "lost decade." It was one of the worst of the last century, with US equities losing a shocking 0.2 percent annually, according to Wilshire Associates. As Rick Ferri pointed out in an interesting *Forbes* article, an investor who embraced a simple asset allocation strategy by diversifying across four classes (US stocks, foreign stocks, bonds, and REITS) and rebalanced to that allocation realized a return of 4.2 percent compounded annually. Like a peloton, the other classes pulled the group ahead while US stocks became exhausted. Although this may not be the most exciting return, for a "lost decade," it isn't too shabby. Asset allocation works.

Why Your Investment Portfolio May Not Be Diversified

(OCTOBER 28, 2011)

Some people think investing is all about picking the right stocks to beat the market. Peter Lynch and Warren Buffett are fabled stock pickers. Wall Street would certainly have you believe this notion because beating the market rings their register. But then investors are told that they should be diversified. Does that mean owning thirty stocks? Which thirty? What's the point?

OWN STOCK MARKETS, NOT STOCKS

Diversification means that you own enough stocks in a market that no one stock can have any major impact on your portfolio. Many brokers buy their clients thirty large companies and declare, "You're diversified!" You know—all the usual big names. How did that work out in 2008 when the largest US companies, including General Motors, General Electric, Citibank, and Bank of America, dominated a portfolio? Not so well. Do you subscribe to Netflix? CEO Reed Hastings was often hailed as the next Steve Jobs—until last July, when Netflix began its fall from $300 per share down to $75 this week—a loss of 75 percent. Big or small, individual companies blow up, and it happens suddenly. Want to minimize the risks that arise when bad things happen to good companies? Own thousands of stocks.

Look inside most mutual funds and you'll see one hundred stocks, but they're there for all the wrong reasons. To be a successful mutual fund manager, you must concentrate your bets on your favorite stocks. It's the only way they have a shot at outperforming the market. But mutual funds with big Netflix positions are underperforming this year, so the typical mutual fund manager figures that he might lose his job trying to be a hero and instead becomes a "closet indexer"—exchanging job security for any chance of beating his market (and justifying his fees).

That's why we only recommend ETFs. They get you stock diversification and save you 80 percent in fees. Want to invest in small American companies? Why pick a few good companies or hire a mutual fund manager? With one ETF, you'll own literally hundreds of stocks. Netflix? Let it crash! You'll never notice.

SPREAD IT AROUND

Consider this: there are other stock markets outside the United States. Germans don't obsess about our Dow. Half of all companies are outside our borders, and world markets tend to move quite independently. Therein lies the second secret of diversification: what causes some to go up often causes others go down.

Markets are the key to successful diversification—the more you have, the better. Diversifying into markets is kind of like creating a prized recipe. Garlic, lemon, oregano, and thyme are not too appetizing on their own, but when skillfully combined with a host of other ingredients, the results can be spectacular.

You want to own a host of diverse markets—and not just safe ones. Horseradish might be dangerous if consumed by itself, but as part of an overall recipe, it delivers positive results. The same goes for adding risky markets. Adding one or two to the mix can have a leavening effect that may actually reduce risk and volatility while adding to overall performance.

US stocks and stocks in Europe, Japan, and Australia tend to move independently from one another, so allocating money to all of these markets creates instant diversification. Emerging markets like China, Russia, India, and Brazil also move to the beat of a different drummer. Bonds and real estate are even further afield from stocks, so adding these markets provides excellent diversification. Every year, some market wins and others lose, and no expert can predict the future. The answer is simple: own them all!

With the proper mix of markets—stocks of large and small US companies, foreign developed countries, emerging markets, US government bonds, real estate, and commodities (using ETFs for each of these markets)—you can consider yourself fully diversified. Now that's a good salad!

Know Your Risk as Well as Your Reward

(JULY 3, 2010)

In competitive pursuits, there are established and transparent measurement systems to determine not just performance but how performance is achieved. In professional sports, a variety of statistics are used to compare individual and team performance. Everyone from team managers to owners and bookies use these common statistics. And because the statistics don't lie, there is little doubt or debate about who is good and why.

With investing (arguably the most competitive and highest stakes game on earth), few understand the stats. Many who have accumulated sizable nest eggs from a lifetime of work understand the RBIs and batting averages of their favorite baseball hero better than they grasp how their money manager is performing.

The most important element of investment performance is risk. You just can't evaluate performance without the context of risk. Many investment advisers sell returns, not risk-adjusted returns. They'll tell you about their favorite manager, who "killed it," but you'll never hear that risks were taken that could have led to the loss of all your money.

Evaluating performance without measuring the amount of risk taken is like looking at a golf score without adjusting for a handicap. The most sophisticated endowment managers and family offices rigorously monitor risk-adjusted performance. They hire the best money managers and monitor levels of risk. They understand how a manager achieves results as clearly as the results themselves.

If your strategy is to actively manage your portfolio, then measuring risk is a vital, complex, expensive, and time-consuming pursuit. How many fund-of-funds invested in Madoff after extensive due diligence and were blindsided by the risks they had taken?

RISK MANAGEMENT SIMPLIFIED

With ETFs, measuring risk is simple. In return for giving up the prospect of outperforming the market, you lower risk, pay lower fees, and statistically outperform most who are paying for performance. In a MarketRiders portfolio you'll never find hidden leverage, quant algorithms predicting market moves, quirky money managers, conflicts of interest, or managers placing large bets with your money.

We measure performance by how efficiently our portfolios deliver returns given the level of risk you were willing to assume. By choosing the right asset allocation and populating your allocations with ETFs, you will get near exact returns for the amount of risk you are willing to take. In 2008, our low-risk portfolios were up because they contained mostly bonds, and our portfolios with large equity allocations were down. The reverse was true in 2009. As we say, it's about as exciting as watching paint dry.

Why You Shouldn't Invest Like Warren Buffett

(MARCH 13, 2010)

Warren Buffett is our generation's Benjamin Franklin—a humble billionaire full of great advice, quips, and invaluable insights.

According to Buffet, most investors should "do as I say, not as I do." The world's greatest investor warns against trying to imitate his stock-picking abilities. For years his unwavering advice has been to buy index funds because (a) very few people have it in their DNA to be great investors, and (b) those who charge you for their investment expertise can rarely outperform the market due to these onerous fees.

In a video lecture to college students, Buffett explained that 99 percent of investors should do what we suggest at MarketRiders, noting that most individuals do not have the talent to invest in individual stocks. He implored his audience to invest in index funds. In his 2005 and 2006 annual reports, Buffett used the imaginary and hilarious fable of the Gotrocks family to parody the insanity of paying fees to professional investment advisers and demonstrate how these fees destroy returns. In 2007, Buffett made a $1 million bet with a leading hedge fund that it couldn't beat the S&P 500 over ten years because of its egregious fees. This bet is posted at longbet.org.

Just because you can pick up a golf club doesn't mean you should bet all your savings on getting on the PGA tour. And just because you (or someone in a suit at an investment management firm) can place a trade with an online broker doesn't mean you can pick winning stocks or mutual funds.

Do as I say, not as I do. Thank you, Warren.

The Law of Compound Returns

(AUGUST 19, 2011)

When the markets get turbulent, investors get emotional. We want to react. Today could be a fear day, but last month there were greed days. On fear days, we react. We wonder, "How much more money can I lose? Should I be getting out?" On greed days, we get excited and, after looking at what we "shoulda, woulda, coulda" done, we get anxious and often buy into a rising tide.

What is the purpose of investing? It sounds like a stupid question, but ask ten investors and you'll get a surprising variety of answers. Is there an answer that allows us to conduct ourselves in a rational way that is not influenced by fear and greed?

Try this out. A recently published biography on the world's most famous investor is titled *The Snowball—Warren Buffett and the Business of Life*. The term *snowball* is a metaphor for a core investment concept: the law of compound returns. Understanding it is critical to your success as an investor and should be at the center of all your investment decisions.

LET IT ROLL

Think of the law of compound returns as a force of nature that describes how wealth grows. A small snowball rolling down a hill will gather weight, increasing its speed and in turn, its size. Wet snow and a long hill are the conditions that turn a snowball into a very large boulder. Continuing with the metaphor, wet snow relates to an investor's rate of return, and the size of the hill is one's time horizon.

TRADING, TAXES, AND FEES

Management fees and taxes dry out wet snow. A small change can mean the difference between having a boulder and having a snowball when you retire. Have you checked the taxes you're paying on your mutual funds? It's probably 1 to 2 percent of your returns because managers turn over all stocks an average of once every eighteen months. Mutual fund charges and broker or adviser fees on portfolios average 2 percent, but index funds and ETFs run about 0.25 percent.

You might not think that's a big difference, but here's how it is. Take a $100,000 portfolio. Using the market's long-term average growth rate of 10.4 percent a year, compounding your gains over twenty years and deducting the 3 percent in fees and taxes, you'd have $287,928 after taxes. But if your fees and taxes were 0.25 percent instead of 3 percent, you would have $607,465. That's over a 100 percent difference! That's double your money based on a difference in fees and taxes of 2.75 percent.

ACCUMULATION IS THE IDEA

How quickly will your money double? Einstein's Rule of 72 says that if you divide your yearly percentage return into seventy-two, you get the number of years it will take to double your money. Let's start with $100,000. If you have a 9 percent return divided into seventy-two, your money will double in eight years ($200,000). In another eight years, you would have $400,000, and so on. But if you get a 6 percent return divided into seventy-two, your money will double every twelve years ($200,000). Within twenty-four years, someone earning 9 percent will have twice as much as someone getting 6 percent.

Here's an answer to the initial question. Your job as an investor is to find a level of risk that you can live with and then structure the most efficient portfolio that delivers a rate of return commensurate with the level of risk you are assuming. Then you must help the law of compound returns work its magic. Your job is not to compete against the stock pickers and market timers on Wall Street—or even hire one to manage your money.

NO ONE CAN GIVE YOU A LONGER HILL

Unfortunately, your age and personal working situation define your time horizon, and these are elements that cannot be changed. But you can keep your snow wet. Taxes, trying to time the market, paying large investment fees, and making investment mistakes interrupt the law of compound returns and lower your returns. They dry out your snow.

When the market has ups and downs, remember that if positioned correctly, your portfolio will grow over time. Capitalism demands a return. Your job is not to react to fear and greed, but rather to stay out of the way, remove the obstacles to the law of compound returns, and let this force work its magic on your money.

Inflation-Proofing Your Portfolio

(MAY 5, 2011)

Inflation is a sneaky pickpocket that slinks into your wallet in the form of higher prices on food, gas, and other necessities, quietly robbing you of wealth. It's the invisible tax—the hole in your water bucket. Because of this, investors are increasingly attentive to the evolving inflation story.

What many investors don't know, however, is the Federal Reserve's dirty little inflation secret. When the Fed reports on inflation, it reports on *core* inflation, a calculation that excludes food and energy costs.

TRICKY NUMBERS

The Fed has not always calculated inflation in this way. In February 2000, it rejected its old method of calculating inflation, which included food and energy, in favor of this new core inflation method, claiming that highly volatile food and energy prices made their influence impractical in determining monetary policy.

When you hear of the inflation rates of the late 1970s, for instance, you are hearing about a number that included food and energy, whereas today's numbers are skewed lower. Similar to how unemployment calculations have been skewed lower using the 1970s method, both inflation and unemployment are higher today than most people realize.

The Fed has clearly shown it wants inflation that is high enough to weaken the US dollar, promote exports, and debase US debt, but also low enough to keep investor confidence high and the economy moving forward. Fed chair Ben Bernanke has stated that the Fed is looking to stoke inflation to a rate of around 2 percent a year.

THE ILLUSION OF FED CONTROL

Unfortunately, inflation is not so easy to control. Inflation has a history of suddenly lurching out of control. Like a careening car that unexpectedly fishtails to one side, driver overcorrection will send the car sliding in the opposite direction. Knowing this, the Fed wants to keep investors calm regarding the inflation story. Just last week, Bernanke suggested that inflation is not a threat and that the US base interest rate will stay close to zero for an "extended period."

What does this mean for you? Historically, developed economies have maintained an inflation rate of around 2 percent and emerging economies have maintained a blended rate of around 6 percent. Strangely, these same economies tend to grow at similar rates.

People who live in emerging economies spend approximately 50 percent of their income on food and energy. In developed economies like the United States, that drops to around 20 percent. Essentially, the poorer you are, the more of your dollars must go to basic needs like food and energy. Therefore, the poor's inflation tax goes up. Sadly, recent inflation of food and energy prices and of other basic commodities, coupled with the deflation of the US dollar, has hit many Americans harder than they may realize.

HOW TO MAKE INFLATION YOUR FRIEND

To respond to the inflation threat, every retirement portfolio should be inflation-proofed. Start by allocating a part of your portfolio to Treasury Inflation Protected Securities (TIPS). TIPS pay a stated dividend, and twice a year , the Consumer Price Index rate—a common measure of inflation—is added to the underlying value (PAR value) of the bond.

Additionally, by adding exchange-traded funds like iShares S&P Global Energy (symbol IXC), iShares Dow Jones US Oil & Gas Ex Index (IEO), and iShares Dow Jones US Oil Equipment Index (IEZ) to your portfolio, you gain diversification to more than three hundred companies impacted by the price of oil and gas.

Finally, add some precious metal exposure to your portfolio through ETFs like SPDR Gold Shares (GLD) or iShares Silver Trust (SLV), both of which will give you low-cost exposure to gold and silver. Beware of farming and food-related ETFs because they involve futures contracts and are unpredictable.

INFLATION AND DEFLATION: BALANCING THE RISK.
Before you run out and turn your entire portfolio into an inflation hedge, remember that like inflation, deflation is also an ever-present risk. Just as quickly as the economy can careen toward inflation, a sudden overcorrection by the Fed can send the economy sliding wildly toward deflation.

Through global diversification and disciplined rebalancing, you can get the inflation pickpocket out of your wallet and rest assured that no matter which way the economy slides, you stand prepared to emerge a winner.

The Flash Crash: Did You Yawn or Did You Freak?

(MAY 15, 2010)

On May 6, 2010, the world was shocked by an unprecedented event—a thousand-point drop in the market in a mere sixteen minutes. During the hours that followed, financial programs on TV and radio featured pundits whose heads were spinning as they sought to comprehend how 10 percent of the market's value could vanish in minutes.

A plethora of explanations quickly followed. We heard about the "fat thumb" scenario, in which a trader was said to have triggered the collapse by selling billions of shares instead of millions by keying in the wrong trade. One of the more interesting speculations was a truly bizarre account involving Nassim Taleb, trader and author of *The Black Swan,* a book that discusses high-impact, impossible-to-predict, rare events that are beyond the realm of normal expectations. According to this grand irony, Taleb's fund placed a sizable S&P short that got the ball rolling for Thursday's violent crash, creating his own "black swan." In the end, the thousand-point drop remains a mystery, and in the absence of any credible and complete explanation, market fear has been resurrected.

WERE YOU AFFLICTED BY TICKER SHOCK?

For those who live by the market's vicissitudes, May 6 was a terrifying roller coaster ride. With each swing of the market, such investors were glued to the ticker, at one moment thrilled and the next gripped by dread. For MarketRiders, such days elicit nothing more than a yawn. With our investments sheltered by a distant time horizon, low fees, and smart diversification, we are free to go about the more important business of our lives. Some investors prefer drama. We prefer peace of mind.

Panic or Steadfast Resolve?

(AUGUST 8, 2011)

In early August 2011, the markets started to dive. The S&P lost all of its gains for the year and more. We were headed for 2008 panic levels.

Everyone is looking for intelligent advice about the recent correction in the global markets. Good luck finding it. You can watch CNBC, read the commentaries, and talk to your neighbor, who loaded up on gold last year. But the truth remains: – markets ebb and flow. They are fickle. They give plentiful returns over long periods of time, but not without big ups and downs.

Markets also move rapidly. In the past ten trading days, the market wiped out nearly a year of gains. Someone saw it coming this week and, if they haven't already revealed themselves, they'll be the letting us know soon. It is almost guaranteed that they'll miss it the next time around, however. That's why we steer you toward ETFs and away from expensive mutual funds that strive to beat the market.

Days like today prove that asset allocation is the number-one decision you can make as an investor. Investing is very personal. We all are different in our incomes, how much we spend, how long we will work, our financial responsibilities, and how much we can deal with risk and uncertainty. What is right for you may not be right for your neighbor. The more bonds you have in your portfolio, the less you are down this month, but the less you made last year. Bonds disappoint the greed in us, but they vindicate the inner "I told you so" during times like these. Our MarketRiders software is designed to determine the right asset allocation for you.

Volatile markets are useful for testing our assumptions. Using new brain-scanning technologies to map how the brain works, psychologists have learned that an investor's perception of gain and loss is not linear. Multiple substantiating studies suggest that the pain associated with a one-dollar loss is twice that associated with the pleasure of a one-dollar gain.

FEEL THE PANIC AND SIT TIGHT

The only intelligent way to handle the emotional aspect of investing and get your allocation right is to understand yourself. It is one thing to feel panicked, but it is another to act on it. If you recently sold a big chunk of your equities or are seriously considering doing so, then you should probably lower your exposure to equities. If you are nervous and upset but sitting tight, they you are probably allocated correctly. One of our investment mentors, Charles Ellis, used skiing as a great analogy in a recent investment journal:

> At…great ski resorts, thousands of skiers are each enjoying happy days, partly because the scenery is beautiful, partly because the snow is plentiful and the slopes are well groomed, but primarily because most skiers choose the well-marked trails that are best suited to his or her skills, strength, and interests. Some like gentle "bunny slopes," some like moderately challenging intermediate slopes, some are more advanced, and still others want to try out trails that are challenging even for fearless experts in their late teens with spring-steel legs. When each skier is on the trail that is right for him or her and skiing that trail at the pace that is right for her or him, everyone has a great day and all are winners.

BALANCING RISK AND RETURN

With MarketRiders, you will have a very low-cost portfolio that is well allocated to global bond and equity markets. Make sure that if you like bunny slopes, you aren't skiing on a double black diamond. If so, dial your portfolio up or down accordingly in terms of bond or equity exposure, and you will get your share of the returns from global capitalism.

Stay the course by rebalancing when you receive our alerts. US equities, Europe, and emerging markets are all down nearly 20 percent since early July, and gold and bonds are doing great. Our system may instruct you to trim gold and bonds and buy more equities, which is counterintuitive and may be difficult, but this is how you buy low and sell high. It has been proven to work over many market cycles.

We're all rattled in this market. Red ink on the screen is hard to watch. But we're ready to rebalance—ready to add to our losers and trim our winners and enjoy the remainder of the summer. We hope you are, too.

Hair on Fire

(DECEMBER 11, 2010)

The end of 2010 was a time of extreme uncertainty that caused even the most sage of investment people to take pause. Deficits... inflation...deflation. Which way would the economy turn—and when? The only thing certain was that nothing was clear.

For those of us who did not live through the Great Depression, there has never been more economic uncertainty. With a scorched-earth economy behind us and numerous land mines before us, betting on trends is harder than ever. For example, half of the soothsayers predict that gold is ready to double, while the other half say it is headed for a plunge. Half say that our bond portfolios will be ravaged by impending inflation, while the other half believe that deflation will make our bonds more valuable. John Bogle declared, "I've never seen a more difficult time to invest, with the specter of these enormous deficits hanging over us, and with the global economy teetering a great deal more than people think…"

Added to Bogle's comments are radical yet opaque tax reform, the backfiring of QE2 efforts, and the eighteen-member deficit commission recommendations that take a serious look at changing even the most sacrosanct government institutions. To make our point, we bring you a small sample of these topics from last week's news. As Yogi Berra once said, "It's tough to make predictions, especially about the future."

HOW WELL ARE YOU SLEEPING?

Those with nest eggs to protect truly face unnerving times. We have a recurring nightmare that grabs us by the throat and drags us, protesting, through a horror-like carnival ride in which we "retire" as eighty-two-year-old Walmart greeters (no offense, but not a fate to which many us aspire).

That's why elite endowments, billionaire families, and sophisticated investors focus on their global asset allocation strategy. We bring their methodology to every investor and allow those who follow our lead not only to survive the madness, but also to find growth through our uncertain future. Exposure to bonds; TIPS; emerging markets; foreign developed stocks; US large, mid, and small-cap equities; gold; and energy makes for a secure portfolio.

Stay the course with your allocations and enjoy peace of mind.

Experts Speak

"The essence of effective portfolio construction is the use of a large number of poorly correlated assets."

—DR. WILLIAM BERNSTEIN, AUTHOR

"On average, 90 percent of the variability of returns and 100 percent of the absolute level of return is explained by asset allocation."

—ROGER G. IBBOTSON AND PAUL D. KAPLAN, ECONOMISTS

"Studies have demonstrated that approximately 94 percent of variability of a fund's investment return is due to asset allocation."

—GARY P. BRINSON, RESEARCHER

CHAPTER 5

Why and How You Should Join the ETF Revolution

"I don't know, I don't care, indexing lets you say those magic words."

—JASON ZWIEG, *WALL STREET JOURNAL*

The MarketRiders investment strategy is based on research that shows that returns are predominantly determined by where your money is invested (your asset allocation). Therefore, investors need a solid allocation plan for all types of available investments, including US stocks, bonds, real estate, and foreign stocks.

ETF stands for exchange-traded fund. Once you decide on your allocations, ETFs are the building blocks you'll use to implement your plan. These are funds that trade on the stock exchange, just like any other stock. You follow the same procedure at your online broker to buy an ETF as you would any stock like IBM or GE. It should cost you between four dollars and ten dollars per trade. ETFs are not a secret, but investment professionals often don't make fees from them, so they go ignored.

Each ETF is a "basket" of stocks that represent a particular index. For example, if you wanted to own every stock in the S&P 500 Index, you would buy one of several ETFs that follow that index, such as SPY or Spiders. By owning one share of SPY, you gain diversification across five hundred stocks.

With ETFs you can invest in practically any market you want. Some of the most popular indexes are the S&P 500 index (tracks the largest US public companies), the Russell 2000 index (tracks some of the smallest US public companies), and the Morgan Stanley Europe Asia Far East (EAFE) index, which is composed of companies in developed foreign countries. ETFs also allow you to invest in real estate, bonds, commodities, sectors, and other markets.

Mutual funds are six to ten times more expensive than ETFs because mutual fund managers hire pros who try to select a few stocks within the index that will beat it. When you invest in an index fund, you basically get the exact returns of the index.

Since computers, and not humans, manage the stocks in an ETF, the fees are very low. MarketRiders portfolios employ the best ETFs based on low fees, high trade volume, and low turnover, all of which reduce taxes.

The Basic Principles of ETF Investing

(AUGUST 22, 2011)

When trying to make sense of the world of ETFs, five simple principles will guide you toward the good and away from the bad and ugly:

1. Index construction. Evaluate each ETF for the quality of the index it tracks and how well the provider replicates the given index's performance over a long period of time. A bad index means a bad ETF.

2. Low management fees. Be sure you are paying rational management fees for the asset class under consideration. In general, the lower your fee, the more you stand to make over time.

3. High volumes. Quality ETFs often average billions of dollars in net assets where daily volumes run very high. This affords sufficient volume and liquidity so that the bid and ask spreads are narrow.

4. Low turnover. More turnover means more taxable income. Look for low-turnover equity ETFs—about 10 percent. Turnover is generally greater for bond ETFs because bonds mature and must be continually replaced.

5. Quality sponsors. Look to Vanguard, iShares, SPDRs, and Schwab ETFs for quality funds. These four firms account for close to 90 percent of all ETF assets and are highly regarded in the industry. Since Vanguard is a not-for-profit institution with the lowest fees in the industry, it tends to keep the other ETF providers honest.

Choosing Only the Best ETFs for Your Portfolio

(SEPTEMBER 11, 2010)

We feel it's important to reiterate that the MarketRiders investment strategy is based on research that shows that returns are predominantly determined by where your money is invested (your asset allocation). Therefore, investors need a solid allocation plan for all types of available investments, including US stocks, bonds, real estate, and foreign stocks.

Once you decide on your allocations (MarketRiders can help with that), ETFs become the building blocks to implement your plan. ETFs are an amazing financial innovation because they give all investors access to the investment strategies used by the most sophisticated investors. They are made possible because of supercomputing technology that enables the instant building and adjustment of baskets of securities for very low fees.

ETFs are the latest investment fad. Heavily advertised by sponsors, the number of available ETFs has grown from nearly seven hundred to over twelve hundred since we launched MarketRiders. Even today, however, only twenty-five ETFs represent half of all assets invested in ETFs. These are the stalwart ETFs that are passively managed baskets that mimic large global indices.

THE NOTION OF FUND PERFORMANCE REVISITED

Many ask, "How is [XYZ] ETF performing?" The question arises from what we call a performance mentality, rooted in years of conditioning from Wall Street. If you have an ETF that mimics the S&P 500, then why ask how it did? Just look at how the S&P 500 did and you'll have your answer.

BEST IN CLASS ETFS

We recommend ETFs that are the best index for a particular asset class. In evaluating ETFs, we ask, "If we look back twenty years from today, will this particular ETF accurately capture, after tax, the performance of its index?" Nearly all of our recommended portfolios include a Vanguard Emerging Markets ETF (VWO), which was up over 76 percent in 2009. We aren't geniuses for having recommended it. It was up because the twenty-eight emerging market economies (Brazil, Russia, India, China, and others) were up almost exactly 76 percent last year. VWO did a good job mirroring this performance.

You can hold and rebalance the ETFs we recommend for a very long period of time and achieve the best after-tax returns.

How to Invest In China without Speaking Mandarin

(OCTOBER 23, 2010)

All MarketRiders portfolios include exposure to emerging market stocks. We want to explain more about this asset class. Stocks in companies in the twenty or so nations included in the popular MSCI Emerging Markets index are dominated by Asia (predominantly Taiwan and Korea) at more than 50 percent, Latin America at 20 percent, Africa and the Middle East at 20 percent, and some smaller European countries. Investing in emerging market stocks is considered high-risk and high return because you own companies in countries that are at an intermediate stage of development. Their economies are still developing and their stock markets are still gaining global clout.

Just because countries like Brazil, India, Russia, and China may be growing at record levels, stock prices don't necessarily rise because their economies and governments are emerging. Shareholders benefit when companies grow after-tax profits. The governments in these countries might have onerous tax rates, state-sponsored price controls, securities laws that are not evolved or enforced, corruption, or risk of wars and violence, to mention a few common risks. All of these elements make these economies and their stock prices highly volatile.

Until a few years ago, the everyday investor had limited access to emerging markets and, when there was an alternative, he or she paid eight to ten times more in fees than institutional and wealthy investors. ETFs have truly democratized international investing. In the past six years, high-priced mutual funds averaging 1.5 percent in annual fees, such as Morgan Stanley Emerging Markets (MGEMX), Lazard Emerging Markets (LZEMX), or T. Rowe Price Emerging Markets (PRMSX), have been challenged by superior low-cost ETFs.

HOW TO COVER THE EMERGING MARKETS

We recommend a single ETF for emerging market stocks: the Vanguard Emerging Markets ETF (symbol VWO). If you owned $10,000 of VWO, you would own a piece of 833 stocks in more than twenty countries for only twenty-seven dollars per year (a 0.27 percent expense ratio). Vanguard trades, rebalances, and maintains this basket of stocks. You won't have to figure out whether China will do better than Russia, or whether you should be investing in Mexico or Thailand. You won't have to decide whether Petroleo Brasileiro is better than China Mobile or Samsung—or pay an arm and a leg to an investment pro to figure this out. With VWO, you'll own them all.

If you want some of your emerging market allocation to include specific countries or continents, there are more specific ETFs. For country and region ETFs, iShares offers EWZ (Brazil), FXI (China), EWY (South Korea), and Latin America (ILF). Expenses for these ETFs range from 0.5 percent to 0.8 percent in fees and are the equivalent of buying the S&P 500 for these countries. Some of our members may use VWO for 80 percent of their emerging markets allocation and then pick two countries for another 5 percent in each. They use the I-want-to-build-it path on the portfolio engine to achieve this.

SHOULD YOU CHOOSE SPECIALIZED ETFS?

Probably not. We advocate a common sense, low-cost, globally diversified portfolio for retirement. For this purpose, there are only twenty or so ETFs that we use at MarketRiders to gain exposure to most asset classes.

How to Buy Two Thousand Businesses In Japan, Europe, and Asia

(FEBRUARY 4, 2011)

Not all foreign stock investments are created equal. A few weeks ago, we wrote about owning stocks in companies based in emerging markets and the different types of risks and returns one could expect. The exciting growth in these countries comes with a fair amount of risk, including governments with onerous tax rates, state-imposed price controls, outdated securities laws, corruption, and risk of wars and violence.

Egypt brings these risks home. If you want to invest in the Egyptian stock market, you can purchase shares of an ETF called the Market Vectors Egypt Index ETF (symbol EGPT), which holds all the important stocks in Egypt. When protests broke out last week, the markets decided that the largest companies in Egypt were worth 25 percent less than they were a day before—and EGPT fell by that amount!

Investing in foreign companies in the twenty-seven developed countries (including the UK, France, Germany, Japan, Australia, and Canada) gives you further diversification and is much less risky. In fact, over long periods of time, these economies perform like the US stock market. Between 1970 and 2004, those stock markets appreciated 10 percent per year, compared with the S&P 500 growth of 11 percent.

WHY OWN FOREIGN STOCKS?

Every retirement investor should own foreign stocks because they reduce risk in a portfolio in two key ways. First, you'll own stocks in other currencies. If the US dollar declines against the yen or the euro, these stocks will appreciate. Second, other countries have unique responses to their own economic circumstances, their governments, their populations, and their tax rates—all of which are different than what happens in the United States. In the 1980s, the experts said Japan was going to take over the world, and its stock market rose 28 percent against the United States, which returned 17 percent. In the 1990s, Japan's markets tumbled and have only recently begun to recover. Demographics can also impact a country and the value of its companies. For example, other countries don't have baby boomers and their populations are aging in different ways.

Owning a basket of developed foreign stocks provides equity ownership that doesn't always have the same fluctuations as US stocks, which reduces risk in a portfolio.

In our MarketRiders retirement portfolios, we allocate about 30 to 35 percent of our equity exposure (not fixed income), to non-US stocks. Most of that allocation goes to developed countries rather than emerging-market countries.

ETFS OR MUTUAL FUNDS?

Investors should own developed foreign country stocks through ETFs instead of mutual funds. The costs are low, and active mutual fund managers statistically don't do better than the indexes they attempt to beat. Also, foreign country mutual funds tend to have very high fees—it's expensive to fly fund managers all over the world to research companies. Instead of paying high fees, buy an ETF that holds all the stocks in all the countries that matter.

We recommend three ETFs in most of our portfolios. By owning shares in Vanguard European ETF (VGK), you own a basket of 481 large companies in sixteen European countries and pay only 0.16 percent in annual fees, which is 10 percent of the cost of comparable mutual funds. Adding Vanguard Pacific ETF (VPL) gives you ownership of 493 large companies in Japan, Australia, Hong Kong, Singapore, and New Zealand. We allocate a small amount to iShares MSCI Canada Index (EWC), which charges 0.53 percent in annual fees.

Here's the best part: with these three ETFs, you don't have to worry about which country will grow faster or whether Toyota will do better than BMW because you will own all of these stocks and capture the growth of these countries and their currencies. As for uprisings, you might sleep better knowing that these countries are at less risk of that occurring.

Strike Oil and Mine for Gold without Getting Your Hands Dirty

(NOVEMBER 6, 2010)

Commodities are one asset class that has recently become acceptable to most financial advisers as part of a globally diversified portfolio. A large number of the most controversial ETFs invest in commodities. Because most commodities ETFs do not perform as advertised, we feel it's important to share our selection process—including which ones we avoid.

A commodity is something for which there is demand, but that is supplied without any real difference across a given market. Commodities prices are determined as a function of their market as a whole. Generally, these are agricultural products, energy, gold and silver, and industrial metals.

HOW THEY CAN HELP YOUR PORTFOLIO

Commodities can be an important hedge against inflation and devaluing currencies. The continuing strong growth in the global economy has created strong demand for a variety of raw materials, from oil to metals and lumber. That demand, in turn, puts upward pressure on the prices of those commodities. Because commodities prices usually rise when inflation is accelerating, they offer protection from the effects of inflation. Few assets benefit from rising inflation, particularly unexpected inflation.

MITIGATING RISK

Commodities have offered superior returns in the past, but they carry a higher risk than most other equity investments. However, by adding commodities that are less volatile to a portfolio of assets, you can actually decrease the overall portfolio risk. That's because commodities have a low correlation to other asset classes.

With such volatility in mind, we add commodities as an asset class on our more aggressive equity-biased portfolios and only invest in commodities that are in permanent limited supply: energy and gold. Our portfolios include the iShares S&P Global Energy Sector (IXC) and SPDR Gold Trust (GLD).

The iShares fund gives you ownership of eighty-six energy companies worldwide—about half in the United States and half in countries such as England, Canada, and China. You'll own the major companies that produce and distribute oil and gas (Exxon, Chevron, Petrochina), as well as those that service the industry (Schlumberger) and others like Murphy Oil and Canadian Oil Sands Trust.

THE PRECIOUS FEW

In the case of gold, silver, and other precious metals, before the advent of ETFs, investors had to own the physical metal. The GLD fund enables anyone to own part of an index based on the physical metal stored in secure warehouses. Most mutual funds charge two to three times more than GLD's 0.4 percent fee. First Eagle Gold (FEGOX) has annual fees of 1.21 percent, and Franklin Gold and Precious Metals (FKRCX) has yearly fees of 1.0 percent.

If you want to stray beyond our model portfolios, consider ETFs like the Energy Select Sector SPDR (XLE), Oil Services HOLDRs (OIH), and iShares Dow Jones US Oil Equipment & Services Index Fund (IEZ), which hold shares of real operating businesses. Also, buy commodity ETFs from only the largest three sponsors: Vanguard, iShares, and State Street (SPDR).

How to Buy the United States

(NOVEMBER 20, 2010)

There are four basic ways investors can use ETFs to invest in US stocks:

1. The lazy way. You can buy one security to own the US stocks that account for most of the value of American corporations. For smaller portfolios, we recommend Vanguard's Total Stock Market ETF (symbol VTI). For an expense of just 0.07 percent per year (that's seven dollars for every $10,000 invested), Vanguard manages a basket of twelve hundred to thirteen hundred US stocks—in just one ETF. Over time, VTI will capture most of the returns of American companies. Because stocks in the basket are allocated based on market capitalization, larger companies will represent the predominant portion of the basket. That's why you might want to try the next method.

2. Three-legged stool. For larger portfolios, we like having the flexibility to lean into small-, mid-, or large-cap stocks so that you can alter your allocations to these groups. For this reason, we recommend three ETFs: the iShares S&P SmallCap 600 Index (IJR), iShares S&P MidCap 400 Index (IJH), and the S&P 500 (SPY). We recommend allocating equally into each of these ETFs. With this method, if you want to weight or underweight one of these groups over time, you can do so.

3. Value and growth believers. For those who like to have some combination of value and growth stocks, you can get even more granular and buy six ETFs to lean heavier in one direction or the other. We recommend Vanguard's Small-Cap Value and Growth ETFs (VBR and VBK), iShares Mid-Cap Value and Growth ETFs (IWS and IWP), and iShares Russell 1000 Large-Cap Value and Growth ETFs (IWD and IWF). Use the same ETF provider in each group—for example, use Vanguard for both small-cap ETFs so that between both, you get all the stocks in the class.

4. Sector players. Select Sector SPDRs divides the S&P 500 into nine sector ETFs so that you can overweight or underweight particular sectors. If you want more exposure to utilities and consumer staples sectors (people need heat and food) and less to financials (you think the banks are still going down), you can allocate accordingly. If you pursue this strategy, get some exposure to all nine of the sectors and add some small-cap and mid-cap exposure using steps two and three above.

PICK A METHOD AND STICK WITH IT

Trading in and out of ETFs creates taxable income, which can eat into returns over time. The magic of ETFs is that if you buy, hold, and rebalance the same ETFs, your savings will grow and you'll be deferring taxes on the increase in value.

Does it matter which method you choose? Over twenty years, it may not. If you are right year after year about your weightings and leanings, then perhaps you can create additional returns.

There are only twenty-eight hundred firms that comprise 95 percent of the value of all public companies in the United States. All of these methods are just another way of slicing and dicing ownership in these same names. By using ETFs, you'll pay an average of 0.20 percent and save yourself 80 percent in costs for similar mutual fund fees. That's worth doing!

How to Own Real Estate without Fixing Toilets

(JANUARY 8, 2011)

Nearly every retirement portfolio should contain real estate holdings. Sophisticated investors hold diversified real estate portfolios that can include portions of office buildings, apartments, industrial warehouses, retail centers, and shopping malls both in the United States and internationally.

Owning real estate has its own set of risks and benefits. A property that is well located and leased gives you debt-like cash flow with the opportunity for appreciation, as with stocks. Leased buildings are valued based upon the stability of cash flow from rents and the cost of replacing the building. Real estate also protects you against inflation, as its value tends to move closely with replacement costs—think land, bricks, concrete, steel, labor, and fixtures. These costs rise with inflation, and landlords raise rents over time if inflation grows.

WHY REITS MAKE SENSE

Most investors don't want to buy a building, however. Fortunately, it's easy to own real estate without ever fixing a toilet or worrying about a roof caving in during a winter storm. You can get a well-diversified real estate portfolio by owning real estate in the form of real estate investment trusts (REITs). These are unique public securities because they pay no taxes and pass 90 percent of their income to investors in dividends. From 1970 to 2009, public REITs returned an average of 9.1 percent per year. That means money invested in REITs doubled every eight years!

That doesn't mean real estate won't have ups and downs. REITs tend to trade in large swings between the fair value of the real estate held in the REIT and the stock price—from a 20 percent discount to a 20 percent premium. Between 2000 and 2009, REITs were up or down by more than 35 percent. But while the stocks may swing, you can sleep at night knowing that you own hard, rent-paying assets.

HOW TO OWN REITS

The best way to own REITs is through an ETF. Why? The costs are low and you'd be hard-pressed to find an active fund manager with the expertise to consistently pick REITs that will beat a REIT index over many years. In fact, owning REITs through a mutual fund can cost you almost 50 percent of the yearly dividend you should receive, in manager fees.

Instead of paying high fees, buy an ETF that holds all the REITs that matter. We recommend two SPDR Dow Jones ETFs in our portfolios to get REIT exposure: the SPDR Dow Jones REIT ETF (RWR), which indexes US real estate, and the SPDR Dow Jones International Real Estate ETF (RWX), which indexes international real estate.

For an annual fee of only 0.2 percent, RWR allows you to own the largest eighty-one REITs in the United States, including the largest American malls such Simon Malls, self-storage units at Public Storage Group, apartments, office buildings, and strip centers. Last year, investors received dividends of 3.61 percent.

For a fee of only 0.59 percent, RWX allows you to own a piece of companies such as the Westfield Group in Australia, which has shopping centers worldwide, and apartments and hotels held outside the United States by Mitsui Fodusan.

Owning REITs using an ETF also gives you global exposure for a low cost and adds diversity to your portfolio. That's why we make sure you have them among your retirement assets.

Why You Should Buy US Treasuries

(APRIL 15, 2011)

In April 2011, the US economy showed signs of further weakening and investors were seeking safe haven. Many doubted the efficacy of buying Treasuries and were losing faith in the US economy as a whole.

TAKE A DEEP BREATH

Everyone knows that inflation is around the corner, the United States is sinking further into debt, and, if you own a bond, it will only go down in value. At some point, the United States is going to have to "pay the piper." The Tea Party may not prevail upon the government to stop spending the country into oblivion.

If you feel anxious just reading these paragraphs, then you understand why the smartest investors in the world don't engage in this conversation. It has always been a bad idea to bet against America and our ability to prosper amid overwhelming difficulties. America will cut back its spending, innovate, and pay off its debts. We will earn our way out. It's just how we do it. Selling Treasuries is a bet against our ingenuity, our work ethic, and our breed of capitalism—which has created more dramatic change in the world over the past century than during any other period in human history.

When deciding how to invest, consider this: actively managed bond funds are the least likely of any funds to beat their benchmarks. A Standard & Poor's study shows that from 2003 to 2008, only 7 percent of bond funds beat their indices. And while Bill Gross has rock-star status, his track record of predictions has been abysmal. Google "Bill Gross new normal" and you will read about one wrong prediction after another since 2009. Gross cares that PIMCO's assets keep growing because they generate over $12 billion per year in fees. Dire predictions in the media bring in new investors.

Large-bond mutual funds control a miniscule portion of the $14 trillion of US debt. The Federal Reserve holds $1.2 trillion, foreign countries hold nearly $5 trillion, and insurance companies, pension funds, and regular investors also hold a fair share of Treasuries. There is no more efficient market than Treasuries, and the Fed has the ability to manipulate it—irrespective of Bill Gross's predictions.

THE REAL REASON TO OWN TREASURIES

Forget the chatter. The critical issue is the function of Treasuries in your portfolio, not whether they should be in your portfolio. While Treasuries generate income, they don't come close to the returns earned from owning equities. From 1925 to 2003, Treasuries appreciated only 5.4 percent per year, or sixty-one times, while large stocks appreciated nearly 10.4 percent per year, or nearly three thousand times. The other price you pay for holding bonds is inflation, which is bad for the long term. While bonds increase in value in a deflationary environment when prices are dropping, this is a rare economic circumstance.

Treasuries protect you against catastrophic events in the world. They are your go-to-sleep-at-night funds. They went up in value after 9/11 and during the 2008 financial crisis. That's why you own them. If you listen to Bill Gross and sell your Treasuries, you'll regret it the next time the sky starts falling.

THE SIMPLE WAY

The best and simplest way to own Treasuries is to buy Vanguard's Total Bond Fund ETF (BND), which is a basket of nearly five thousand bonds and yields more than 3 percent a year. Worried about inflation? The average duration of all the bonds is only five years. Only 8 percent of these bonds have durations greater than twenty years, and 25 percent are between one and three years. BND consists of 43 percent Treasuries, 28 percent US-guaranteed mortgages, and about 5 percent foreign bonds. The rest is investment-grade corporate bonds. For Vanguard to buy, hold, and rebalance, the annual fees are a paltry 0.12 percent.

Next time your heart palpitates as you read that owning Treasuries is a bad idea, consider the source and the function they have in your portfolio.

The Other Kind of TIPS: Inflation Protection

(NOVEMBER 27, 2010)

In January 1997, the US government began issuing a new type of bond: Treasury Inflation Protected Securities (TIPS). TIPS are a separate asset class that's distinct from bonds because these securities behave differently during inflationary times. By owning them, you are further diversifying your portfolio and reducing risk. If you don't own TIPS, you should. At MarketRiders, every retirement portfolio we recommend has at least a 5 percent allocation to TIPS.

Here's why: regular bonds depreciate in value if there is inflation. If you bought a $100,000 bond that pays 5 percent interest, you'd get $5,000 per year in interest. But if in three years, bonds were paying 8 percent interest, the bond you owned would be worth less because investors would only have to buy a $62,500 bond to get the same $5,000 yearly payment.

TIPS protect you from inflation because the amount you get at maturity is adjusted for any inflation that occurred while you owned it. Think of TIPS as a bet with the government. If there is inflation, the government will add the Consumer Price Index to the value of your bond. The coupon interest rate is constant, but it generates a different amount of interest when multiplied by the inflation-adjusted principal, which is how you are protected against inflation. Of course, if there is deflation, then your principal is reduced, but this is a rare economic circumstance. TIPS are offered in 5-, 10- and 30- year maturities.

HOW TIPS HAVE PERFORMED

During the past five years, while there has been little to no inflation, TIPS have appreciated about 5.2 percent per year compared with an index of the total bond market, which has returned 6.3 percent. Had there been rampant inflation during the past five years, you'd have been happier owning TIPS.

ETFs are the best way to own TIPS. You don't have the hassle and cost of buying mutual funds, you can invest any amount that you wish, and you can buy shares for the cost of buying any stock through your online broker. Some investors go through the cumbersome process of purchasing TIPS directly from the US Treasury, but your selection is limited. Other investors flock to such funds as BlackRock's Inflation Protected Bond, for which they pay 1.63 percent in fees—more than the interest paid on the bonds themselves! Almost all funds that invest in TIPS hold about thirty to thirty-three bonds with a similar average duration of five years.

We're all worried about QE2, government spending, and the diminishing value of our money when inflation kicks in.

MarketRiders portfolios give you a bet with the US government so that it can pay you for inflation.

ETFs and Taxes?

(JANUARY 15, 2011)

While the über wealthy use exotic tax strategies to exploit esoteric loopholes, the everyday investor has one great tax trick available in the form of exchange-traded funds. ETFs offer a modern-day tax miracle. Sure, when it comes to capital gains from the sale of an ETF, investors must give Uncle Sam his slice of the pie. But as a highly tax efficient, long-term investment vehicle, ETFs have a sophisticated architecture that, when it comes to taxes, leaves their mutual fund brethren looking a bit haggard.

THE TAX BASICS

First, some tax basics for all types of funds: when you make a profit, you have to pay the government capital gains tax. Capital gains rates differ depending on whether the asset is held less or more than a year, creating short- or long-term gains. These tax rates vary depending on an investor's income level, but generally, federal tax rates under the Bush-era tax plan can be as high as 15 percent for long-term and 35 percent for short-term capital gains. State taxes also apply.

Most ETFs also generate dividends that are taxed. By meeting a specific set of holding criteria, long-term ETF investors will predominantly enjoy qualified dividend tax rates up to 15 percent, with the exception of funds that track real estate investment trusts (REITs), which are unfortunately taxed as ordinary income. While both ETFs and mutual funds can generate capital gains, the tax implications of each are significantly different.

MUTUAL FUNDS ARE TICKING TIME BOMBS

Imagine if everyone in your neighborhood filed a joint tax return. What if your neighbor, Joe, sold his business and you were required to pay a portion of his tax? Not acceptable, you would say.

Unfortunately, that is how mutual fund investing works. If one investor in the fund sells their position, the fund manager must sell underlying stock to give that investor's money back. That underlying stock may have a very low tax basis because it was added to the fund years before you invested. As a participant in the fund, you get hit with a portion of the tax consequence of the other person's sale.

TAXES: A REAL DRAG

This mutual fund tax bomb grows daily and will eventually explode when rebalancing and redemptions force these low cost-basis shares to be traded. There have been instances where a mutual fund manager has held an underlying equity for years, accruing significant capital gains, only to eventually sell and foist a portion of the tax burden onto the new shareholder.

That's why looking at a mutual fund's published performance is an inadequate measure for an investment decision. And unfortunately there's little visibility of the size of the boat anchor the fund is dragging in the form of excess taxes.

ETF TAXES WORK DIFFERENTLY—AND BETTER

As individual investors buy and sell shares of an ETF, a supercomputer-enabled arbitrage happens in the blink of an eye between the ETF provider and the middleman. Your shares are combined with the shares of other buyers and sellers that are traded for the underlying equities with the fund itself. In this way, individual investors never directly buy underlying taxable shares. This method allows the ETF provider to manage the tax bill for investors. In fact, this methodology is so effective that it is rare for an ETF to generate any taxable income at all.

Additionally, the cost basis of the underlying equities within the ETF is constantly being reset upward and at arm's length from the individual investor. The result is wonderful. The ETF behaves like an individual equity in terms of taxes, but enjoys the diversification of a mutual fund—the best of both worlds.

For these reasons, ETFs are growing. In 2008, Morningstar conducted a survey on capital gains distributions for ETFs across twenty-seven broad-based indexes over five-, ten- and fifteen-year horizons. The study showed that only two ETFs made capital gain distributions over the past five years, while just one ETF made distributions over the past ten years.

Dumping your old mutual funds in favor of the more sophisticated and tax-efficient architecture of ETFs is like tossing out the old Motorola flip phone in favor of a new 4G smartphone. The technology is simply better. Along with low fees and reliable performance, tax efficiency is another reason to get on the ETF bandwagon. You will be glad you made the change.

Picking ETFs: the Good, the Bad and the Ugly

(MARCH 12, 2011)

In the mid 1990s, exchange-traded funds came riding down Wall Street like Clint Eastwood in an old spaghetti western—fearless and ready to take on the bandits who had been terrorizing the townsfolk. For years prior to the arrival of ETFs, average investors were held hostage by obscene fees while mutual fund robbers brashly collected their booty, threw back some expensive whiskey, and then shamelessly shot up the town.

The first ETF—Index Participation Shares—came to the rescue in 1989. This S&P 500 proxy traded on the American Stock Exchange but was quickly gunned down by the Chicago Mercantile Exchange, which quickly perceived the threat. It wasn't until 1993 that the real gunslinger rode into town and changed the order of the fund industry forever.

THE RIGHT IDEA

In 1993, SPDR S&P 500 (symbol SPY) was launched on the New York Stock Exchange. Known as SPDRs or Spiders, the fund became the largest ETF in the world. In just over fifteen years, there are now close to one thousand ETFs with more than $1 trillion in assets, and they are growing at a breakneck pace of nearly 30 percent year over year. This is the kind of ETF to own.

Just when ETFs were winning the day, the ETF industry drifted from its sound mooring after the SEC approved a redefinition of the term *index* in 2003. Before then, ETFs were limited to holding baskets of stocks that tracked broad market indices such as the S&P 500 or MSCI EAFE for foreign-developed country markets. After 2003, the SEC allowed ETF providers to create any set of guiding rules to form newfangled indices. This changed the definition of an index and allowed the Wall Street crowd to run wild and create the latest, greatest index du jour, cluttering the universe of good ETFs with a never-ending wave of convoluted, bad, and, in some cases, downright ugly ETFs.

THE BAD AND THE UGLY ETFS (AVOID THESE)

With new indexes popping up daily, the original purity of ETFs as suitable building blocks for asset allocation has been polluted.

One of the most extreme examples ~~of this~~ is an ETF released in 2007 (now closed) by FocusShares, which developed an index of mid- and large-sized companies consisting of casinos, producers of beer and malt liquors, distillers, vintners, and cigarette manufacturers, and called it a "sin" index. Below is a list of potentially bad and ugly ETF categories to watch out for.

LEVERAGED ETFS

After ProShares launched the first leveraged ETFs, a wave of leveraged products followed. Strangely, these leveraged products have been known to severely miss the index over the long haul. Because daily returns are compounded, the returns of leveraged ETFs over periods longer than one day are likely to differ in amount. And leverage is dangerous. Take, for instance, Direxion Daily Financial Bear 3X Shares (symbol FAZ), which plunged 95 percent, earning it the ignominious title of worst performing ETF in 2009.

ACTIVELY MANAGED ETFS

You know the old saying, "If you can't beat 'em, join 'em"? Well, this seems to be the case with many active money managers, who are now moving their practices from the mutual fund industry over to the ETF space. ETFs with a portfolio manager face the same challenges faced by mutual funds—high fees and poor long-term performance records.

COMMODITY ETFS

These hold futures contracts. Avoid ETFs that buy futures contracts to achieve commodity exposure. Futures-based funds can fail to track their target index and are vulnerable to problems such as contango and backwardation. It is best to avoid such

ETFs and stick with commodity ETFs that actually hold the underlying assets.

KEEP YOUR PORTFOLIO SANITIZED

For you investment geeks who want a more comprehensive discussion on how we've picked the ETFs for our MarketRiders portfolios, go to marketriders.com. When it comes to ETFs, invest in the good and avoid the bad and ugly. As tempting as newfangled ETFs can be, the details reveal serious investment risks. By sticking with the five principles for finding good ETFs, you can invest with confidence knowing that you have kept the bandit out of your portfolio.

Experts Speak

"The best way to own common stocks is through an index fund..."

—WARREN BUFFETT, BERKSHIRE HATHAWAY, INC.

"Most of my investments are in equity index funds. Why pay people to gamble with your money?"

—WILLIAM F. SHARPE, NOBEL LAUREATE, STANFORD UNIVERSITY

"The only way to 'beat an index' is to invest in something other than the index. Why would you, when the only source of long-term risk and return data is the index? Since you can't beat the index, be the index."

—MARK HEBNER, INVESTMENT ADVISOR

CHAPTER 6

How to Really Buy Low, Sell High, and Lower Risk

"Rebalancing your portfolio will increase your long term returns... this is an effective way of becoming a contrarian, always moving in the opposite direction of the crowd."

—DR. WILLIAM BERNSTEIN, ECONOMIST

Have you noticed how investors want to hold the winning stock and sell the losers? It's common sense, right? Get rid of the junk and acquire more of what is working. If you doubt this fact, look at the bubble and burst cycles of dotcom stocks and real estate. Unfortunately for the average investor, the good old double down philosophy seems to rule the day.

Everyone, from your day-trading buddy to the kid hocking Pokémon cards, knows that the first rule of investing is to buy low and sell high. Strangely, when you analyze the psychology of chasing winning stocks, you learn that it is a buy high and sell low investment practice. When a stock is soaring to the skies, investors pile in, because obviously it is a winner. Sooner or later, however, some unforeseen event forces the stock south. Sometimes the market itself begins to collapse. For the undisciplined investor, the pain increases and eventually becomes unbearable. Like a kid pinned down by a bully, the investor eventually squeals "uncle" and sells his position in order to run for safety. The tragic boom–to-bust cycle is complete.

In comparison, sophisticated investors build on their strict asset allocation methods via ongoing and disciplined portfolio rebalancing. As asset classes move cyclically, the sophisticated investor will do the hardest thing in portfolio management—sell winners and buy losers. In this way, the investor is locking in profits from the outperforming asset classes and positioning the portfolio for future growth when the underperforming asset classes cycle back. This is what it really means to buy low and sell high—rebalance with unflinching certitude. One of Warren Buffets famous quips is that he "gets fearful when others are greedy and gets greedy when others are fearful." He buys low and sells high. Through clearly defined portfolio targets and courageous rebalancing, you can do the same.

Having the Guts to Stay the Course

(JUNE 12, 2010)

The MarketRiders system of buy, hold, and rebalance is an investment approach based on solid research and unshakable facts. We can never remove all doubt, but we've harnessed the most scientifically verifiable investment approach known today. Rebalancing adds to returns and helps manage risk. You maintain your target allocations and the risk level you set for yourself when you built your portfolio. Riding winners is fun, but what goes up certainly comes down. Using the casino analogy, rebalancing forces you to take money off the table and add to losing bets that will be tomorrow's winning ones.

It's tough to maintain your allocations, and trimming a gold position or buying Europe while it is apparently swirling down the toilet is not easy. At moments like these, lean into the facts, push back your emotions, and rebalance your portfolio. You will be glad you did.

Rebalancing: Eating the Peas in Your Portfolio

(SEPTEMBER 18, 2010)

As a young child I had an ongoing battle with my mother over eating my peas. It may have related to the fact that the peas she served came from a Del Monte can and were pale and overcooked, or possibly from my ubiquitous childhood disdain for anything green. Whatever the reason, the peas had to be eaten before I could leave the table, so I choked them down.

Portfolio rebalancing faces the same disdain from many investors. Why would an investor want to sell equities that are outperforming and buy others that are underperforming? Just like a mother who will not allow her child to live on dessert alone, a smart retirement investor accepts rebalancing as an irreplaceable discipline that results in portfolio health.

How to Invest During a Weak Growth Economy

(JUNE 3, 2011)

In late spring 2011, the US economy hit a major stall, with slow going ahead for what appeared to be months, if not years. What was an investor to do besides read the billboards and inhale CO_2?

The news is in. Manufacturing growth crept to its slowest pace in twenty months, with the index of manufacturing activity experiencing its biggest decline since 1984. Payrolls were shockingly, weak according to ADP, and a mere 38,000 jobs were added in May, down from 177,000 in April. Sadly, this is not just a US problem. This month's manufacturing reports from China, Russia, Poland, Hungary, and Japan indicate that they were all down, with more underwhelming data expected as the month of June rolls on.

This is the moment when the anxious investor begins to panic. Last year it was all about rising stock prices, commodity investments, and the emerging market boom. Now economists are talking about extended weak growth and how we have kicked the debt can down the road and now must pay. So what should an investor do? Is it time to change lanes—to move from one overly weighted allocation model to the next in search of economy-defying returns?

REBALANCING FOR THE LONG HAUL

An investor who is constantly shifting allocations in search of returns is similar to a stressed-out driver trying to make her way down Interstate 405, the nation's busiest stretch of highway on a Friday afternoon before a holiday. Traffic is at a near standstill, but the driver is determined to get to her destination on time in spite of the fact that some 320,000 other drivers are trying to do the same.

This harassed driver seeks to dart from one lane to the next in the hope of finding some small advantage. Her lane grinds to a crushing halt while the drivers four lanes over seem to be effortlessly slipping by. With great consternation, the driver slowly but determinedly works her way over, one lane at a time, rudely nosing her vehicle into tiny spaces to reach the sought-after lane of freedom.

For a few brief moments a wave of satisfaction washes over the driver as she hits her accelerator and pops up from five to thirty miles per hour, finally passing that old lady who had crept along in front in the silver Camry, oblivious and out of touch. But then it happens. Her new lane grinds to a sudden and dangerous halt. She is at a standstill. The frustration builds. Then, as she looks to her left, she notices that the lane from whence she came is now moving freely. As she tries to creep her way back, right there before him the silver Camry slips by, the happy old lady smiling away, at peace in the midst of the 405 storm.

DRIVING HOME A POINT

This driving metaphor provides an interesting allegory for investing behavior. Globally diversified investors participate in an industry with millions of hardworking men and women and experience growth in companies and economies. Sometimes these economies enjoy stretches of unfettered growth that is celebrated and enjoyed by all—not dissimilar to flying down the 405 on a Sunday morning. Then there are times when these businesses and economies become cramped and overburdened. Growth painfully slows as these economies right themselves from a traffic jam.

The wise investor learns that these patterns are essential and expected components of all economies that should not have much effect on investment patterns. By accepting the simple fact that she cannot outperform the market, the wise investor can rest at ease knowing that a well-diversified portfolio will reap a reward. Like the happy old lady on the 405, this investor is not thrilled that the economies are moving slowly, but is happy because her plan accounts for slowdowns and she knows that they, too, will pass.

MOST DETOURS ARE SHORT-LIVED

The wise investor accepts that disruptions are part of the investment journey. Although she enjoys years of high, double-digit returns, she accepts that her portfolio will also move slowly at times. There is no need to change lanes. Making significant changes to a portfolio's allocation is expensive and usually unfruitful. Tax friction and trading costs burden such lane-changing investors with a disadvantage that must now be overcome with dramatically increased growth. Once such an investor adjusts her allocation, as we saw this week, the news hits, economists speak, and it is time once again to make more changes.

During periods of slow growth, each investor has a choice. She can chase after the fast-moving lane, or jump from one allocation to the next, in search of a miracle, or she can accept the seasonal slowdown, trust her allocations, turn on her favorite radio station and, like the old woman on the 405, enjoy the journey.

Herd Mentality: Are You Chewing the Cud?

(JUNE 16, 2011)

It appears that the Delphic oracles have emerged from the modern-day temple of Apollo (that being Wall Street) to share their wisdom. What is their sage advice, you may ask? Sell! Sell your stocks and hunker down in a more defensive position.

The numbers are in: employment growth is down, real estate is down, manufacturing is down, there are debt problems at home, and there are debt problems abroad. The financial pundits have come forth from their glass-towered temples to offer counsel. Like well-behaved cattle, the mooing masses have left their fair pastures and are being herded through the rancher's gate to some unknown destination that will provide the hoped-for, upgraded cud for the chewing. Or might it be the slaughterhouse?

HERD MENTALITY

It is well researched and highly documented by philosophers such as Søren Kierkegaard and Friedrich Nietzsche, scientist Wilfred Trotter, psychologists Freud and Jung, and economist Thorstein Veblen, to name only a few. It is easily seen in investing through cyclical frenzied buying (bubbles) and frantic selling (crashes) in the stock market. These sudden swings are rooted in irrational investing practices and driven by emotion—greed in bubbles and fear in crashes.

New economic data is acted upon within seconds by leading portfolio managers armed with cutting-edge, rapid-response technology. These in-the-know active managers move the market. Then the media reports, and articles grace the front page of national publications and hit the headlines of primetime television. Jim Cramer starts banging his toys and yelling, "Sell, sell, sell!" The frenzy is afoot.

PLENTY OF MOOING

Six straight weeks of market losses have not been seen since 2002, and this event has pushed the Dow Jones Industrial Average below 12,000 after an exuberant eight-month run in which corporate profits and share prices soared. Just when the retirement accounts of ordinary Americans were beginning to look healthy again, bang! We are thrust back into dark times.

And, boy, does this type of news preach! This is when the herd really gets moving. Investment advisers are inundated with bleating customers asking to be moved into defensive positions. With herd-like agility, these investors have a knack for timing the lows with perfect precision. Never mind the fact that the system is rigged to slaughter slow-moving cattle that make their moves a bit too late. Year after year, these retail investors are easily rounded up for the slaughter by pros who know how to make a real profit.

Investors forget the fact the stocks do not rise steadily over time. They do so in a rather abrupt series of fits and starts, with a few days of large gains sprinkled randomly throughout the year. According to finance professor H. Nejat Seyan, if you missed the ninety best-performing trading days from 1963 to 2004, your annual returns plummeted from 11 percent to 3 percent. You would need to be an oracle to accurately pick the ninety best days out of 14,694!

Suffering from collective irrationality, these investors are like sheep without a shepherd, lacking any sense of long-range vision or the guiding principles to anchor their portfolio management. They are exposed and ready to become prey. They are ships without moorings. Their portfolios are tossed to and fro in the market's choppy seas.

THE HERD COULD BE MISGUIDED

The first lesson of Wall Street is to exploit mass-market psychology by acting in a contrarian fashion. Studies by economists and psychologists have found that investors are most influenced by recent events—market news, political events, earnings, and so on—and ignore long-term investment and economic fundamentals.

As a retirement investor, you have a few clear and simple choices. You can enter the active management fray and compete with the big dogs, you can follow the masses and fall prey to the bloodletting, or you can rise above it all by rooting your investment philosophy in proven science and long-range planning. Driving fees mercilessly down and embracing basic global asset allocation and contrarian rebalancing will deliver you from cud chewing and into a zen-like peace. Instead you can rule your portfolio with long-range and academically proven principles and invest effectively with peace of mind.

Bond With Your Bonds

(JANUARY 29, 2011)

Inflation hit the headlines. European equities were heading south. Buffet declared bonds history. Had the bond bubble gone bust? What was a wise investor to do? Say goodbye to treasuries—then what?

As investment advisers, it seems that we have a daily conversation with an investor who is running for the exit with whatever is getting trashed in the media. Last April it was European equities. This month it has been bonds. The prognosticators have spoken, and apparently the news has finally leaked out to the masses: inflation is either here or just around the corner, and with it the great and terrible day of reckoning for bonds. Yes, a dotcom-sized bubble has inflated the bond market before our very eyes, leaving only the most foolish among us still holding on to our bonds. When the bond market finally craters, it will be the stubborn few that the punishment pigs, as they say, and deserve slaughter.

The consensus for fleeing bonds has become more powerful with each passing week. The first notable warning shot came from Warren Buffett at his annual Berkshire Hathaway meeting when he predicted the future demise of the bond market. Soon after, the Vanguard Group announced worries about bond instability. Journalists, economists, and wealth managers have joined in chorus proclaiming disaster in the bond market. With such a dire consensus, why would any investor still buy bonds?

WHY BUYING BONDS MAKES SENSE

For the principled retirement investor, bonds are a critical asset class in a well-diversified portfolio. Much like a rock band that needs lead, rhythm, and bass guitars backed by drums, a retirement investor needs a bond allocation to make his portfolio sing. All the elements of a retirement portfolio work together to make beautiful investment music. Each asset serves to help returns or mitigate risk in an atmosphere of intelligent skepticism about economic predictions. This approach dictates that it may be time to rebalance your portfolio by trimming equities that are flying high and buying a few more bonds.

One idea investors should understand is what we call the Third Newtonian Law of Economic Motion: for every economist, there is an equal and opposite economist. You don't have to look far to find great minds lining up on the side of a long deflation wave fueled by a mind-boggling backlog of massive debt. Take Jan Hatzius, Goldman Sachs's chief US economist, who has been nothing short of shrill in warning of the severe deflationary risk still facing America and the world. Furthermore, according to a National Association for Business Economics survey, 30 percent of its members still believe deflation is our primary risk for the next five years. Although no longer the majority view, deflation is still a concern for many.

Now consider John Mauldin, who publishes one of the nation's leading financial newsletters. Last week he cited Gary Shilling's predictions for 2011 in his annual investment strategies article entitled "9 Buys, 9 Sells." Shilling's first and most emphatic recommendation is, of all things, to buy bonds! Shilling passionately lays out eight arguments, from the hard landing of the Chinese economy to the US suffering a Japan-like malaise, all in favor of bonds as an outperforming asset class for the next five years.

Should one buy or sell bonds? The answer lies in one's philosophy toward investing. If an investor is a long-term and principled retirement investor, he or she can escape the clamor of mass hysteria by sticking to a disciplined approach that rises above such frays. Will inflation or deflation rule the day? The principled investor humbly answers, "I don't know." Today it looks as though we are leaning toward inflation. Tomorrow, there may be news about a country or state defaulting, China's inflation rate running rampant, or some other disruptive event that could send deflationary fears toward the ceiling. Yesterday's news in Egypt sent investors back to bonds. Go figure!

Investing's Uncool: Losing Your Money!

(SEPTEMBER 4, 2010)

The renowned 1970s funk band Tower of Power raised an all-important question about coolness in their hit "What is Hip?" "What is hip, tell me tell me if you think you know," the band wailed, pondering a subject that grips many in our pop-driven culture.

In his book *The Tipping Point: How Little Things Can Make A Big Difference,* Malcolm Gladwell explores how products, people, and ideas move from unknown to cool and back again. Gladwell offers a unique premise whereby people he calls connectors define what is cool for mavens, who in turn popularize the new fad with salesmen, who take the message to the world. Through this process, products, services, and fads can suddenly be thrust from obscurity to cool.

Take, for example, Crocs sandals, which became the rage with pro athletes and movie stars. These cultural icons shamelessly donned strange pink rubber slippers. In the blink of an eye, Crocs were suddenly hip. Croc kiosks offered a wide array of colors and sizes and became ubiquitous in airports, malls, and retail outlets to cater to kids, moms, and business people alike.

One day someone ran into George, their profoundly uncool neighbor, who was wearing his neon-green Crocs. For some reason, they just didn't look the same on George—who was pale and out of shape and wearing shorts several dreadful inches above his knees—as they did on Kobe Bryant. Crocs were done. The uncool to cool and back again cycle had transpired before our eyes.

KEEP YOUR COOL: REBALANCE REGULARLY

Unfortunately, investment strategies also go through waves of cool and uncool. When we started MarketRiders, we knew that our biggest marketing challenge would be its lack of cool. How could an investment philosophy that replaces the casino-like thrill investing with a sane, buttoned-up institutional method ever compete with the daily fun and excitement of a Jim Cramer?

Gladwell's process seems to be taking hold and low-cost investing seems to be getting…well, cool. New websites launch every month touting the merits of the MarketRiders approach. Schwab, Fidelity, and Vanguard are actively swapping investors out of expensive mutual funds and into ETFs.

The fact is, we don't care. We do not promote the MarketRiders approach because it is the newest media fad or investment idea to be crowned as vogue by the financial hipsters. We follow these principles because they are rooted in empirical investment research and have survived decades of rigorous testing in the furnaces of institutional portfolio management.

Cool or uncool, we'll keep wearing our version of pink Crocs not because Kobe wears them or because our neighbor George does not. No, we stay faithful to our approach because we love how this pair of sandals fits.

Crocs are the official shoes of MarketRiders. Go to market-riders.com and send us an email. We may have a few extra pairs on hand.

Experts Speak

"We can extrapolate from the study that for the long-term individual investor who maintains a consistent asset allocation and leans toward index funds, asset allocation determines about 100 percent of performance."

—ROGER IBBOTSON, ECONOMIST

"History shows that a thoughtfully designed, diversified allocation of 'passive' funds typically beats all but a few active managers. It's not easy to structure and maintain such a strategy. It requires some initial research and discipline to stay the course. But it's much easier than predicting which active managers will randomly beat this approach."

—EUGENE FAMA, NOBEL LAUREATE, UNIVERSITY OF CHICAGO

CHAPTER 7

Greed, Fear, and Portfolio Breakdowns

A market is on fire. Jump in or miss out. Every Dow stock is down. Time to bail? Many people invest with their emotions. Greed and fear are the emotions most hazardous to investors. But in truth, emotions in general are not helpful in making investment decisions. Maybe it's because markets behave irrationally. They are certainly impossible to predict. One thing is clear: investors who do really well over time put emotions aside and turn to their left brains. In this chapter we look at how emotions play into investment decisions and how calmness, planning, and prudent action may serve you better.

How to Manage Your Investment Anxiety

(AUGUST 26, 2011)

As uncouth as it may be, worrying about one's investments seems to be the order of the day. It's no wonder: as the markets careen to and fro, publications are replete with stories of advisers and Wall Street pros dumping their stocks in favor or bonds and cash as they scurry to the sidelines.

As usual, the average retirement investor is caught off balance and feels a few steps behind the curve. What is an investor to do? It does feel a bit like 2008 again, doesn't it? Is it too late to take a cue from the pros, pull up stakes on a long-term investment mentality, and find a nearby bunker to hunker down in with a bag of bonds that are now returning less than the rate of inflation?

At times like these, simple positive thinking doesn't extract the thorn of worry from the back of the investor's mind. In spite of conjuring up Bobby McFerrin's "Don't Worry, Be Happy" chorus or humming a bar of "Hakuna Matata," the worry still creeps in at unexpected moments like a terrible and relentless rot.

However, investment anxiety can be tamed. The key is having a clear understanding of what should and should not be on your list of worries. Let's begin with what not to worry about: the direction of the markets.

I DON'T KNOW AND I DON'T CARE

Famous financial columnist Jason Zweig once wrote powerfully about how index investing liberates the investor from the anxieties of trying to predict market movements. His words from 2001 are as relevant today as they were then:

> Indexing enables you to say seven magic words: "I don't know, and I don't care." Will value stocks do better than growth stocks? I don't know, and I don't care—my index fund owns both. Will health care stocks be the best bet for the next twenty years? I don't know, and I don't care—my index fund owns them. What's the next Microsoft? I don't know, and I don't care—as soon as it's big enough

> to own, my index fund will have it, and I'll go along for the ride.
>
> Indexing enables me to say, "I don't know, and I don't care," liberating me from the feeling that I need to forecast what the market is about to do. That gives me more time and mental energy for the important things in life, like playing with my kids and working in my garden.

When it comes to worrying, one should only worry about what can be controlled. Although countless people have tried to control the public markets through hours of mental consternation and sleepless nights, markets rarely, if ever, obey. Therefore, the current vagaries of the market need to be ignored in exchange for the science of long-range planning based on cold, hard investment facts. It may seem like the world is falling into a hole, but investment science indicates otherwise.

Those who have the courage to ride the markets through ups and downs and hold their course over decades will be handsomely rewarded.

I DO KNOW AND I DO CARE

There are some aspects of investing that actually are worthy of the serious retirement investor's attention. Two elements within the intelligent investor's control are asset allocation and investment costs.

While millions of Americans tune into Jim Cramer's *Mad Money* to watch him race about with shrieks, squeaks, and squeals, proclaiming what stock to buy or sell, the intelligent investor understands that the research is conclusive. Ninety percent of investment returns are rooted in asset allocation, not stock picking. The intelligent investor focuses energy on identifying six or seven asset classes with as little correlation as possible: US equities, foreign developed stocks, emerging markets, commodities such as gold and energy, real estate investment trusts, inflation-protected Treasuries, bonds, and possibly more.

The investor then works carefully to identify, based on individual risk tolerance, time horizon and other factors and the appropriate mix of these asset classes for his or her portfolio. Once the portfolio is constructed, the investor rigorously maintains allocations over the years, making adjustments only when needs dictate investment policy changes, not because Cramer bonked his bonker or because of any other market madness.

Finally, the intelligent investor overcomes investment anxiety by driving all unnecessary investment costs far from the portfolio. While market movements cannot be controlled, costs can be. Therefore, the investor makes sure to use low-cost index funds and ETFs as essential building blocks for a diversified portfolio. Instead of paying one to one-and-a-half points for mutual funds, the intelligent investor is able to achieve global diversification for around one fifth of 1 percent annually.

Additionally, by removing all unnecessary intermediaries that stand between investor and money invested, agency risk is dramatically reduced. The investor no longer needs to fret that some money manager is going to go AWOL with hard-earned retirement dollars or fear becoming an unwilling participant in the next episode of the ongoing Wall Street saga of investor meets crook.

Like Wilkie Collins, the famous English novelist, once said, "Peace rules the day when reason rules the mind." By accepting your inability to control or predict the markets, and embracing your ability to drive down fees and construct wise allocations, you, too, can shirk Wall Street madness and say goodbye to investment anxiety.

Portfolio Envy: Why Her Portfolio is Bigger Than His:

(OCTOBER 30, 2010)

While Freud's 1908 theory of penis envy has been wrought with controversy for over a century, the financial sciences have clearly demonstrated that when it comes to money management, most men should have a serious case of portfolio envy. For men who take pride in bringing home the bacon, this realization could be quite emasculating. But research by economists Dr. Terrance Odean and Dr. Brad Barber has revealed that women's risk-adjusted returns outpace those of men by 1 percent annually. Additionally, a past National Association of Investors Corporation study corroborates this finding and even suggests a wider gender gap, with women outperforming men by a whopping 1.4 percent annually.

MINIMIZING RISK

One of the difficulties faced by male investors is the testosterone factor—an innate urge to beat the other guy and then, of course, to brag about it. This may explain why men trade in their accounts 45 percent more than women. While many men may feel that getting one's panties all wadded up over a little bit of risk is unnecessary, research shows that sober risk analysis is essential to constructing a well-diversified portfolio and achieving long-term performance.

For whatever reason, minimizing risk doesn't come naturally for men. A recent New York City Department of Transportation study revealed that men are 40 percent more likely to speed through a yellow light than women. Tragically, a 2007 TrafficSTATS report revealed that men have a 77 percent higher risk of dying in a car accident.

Men run red lights in other areas of life as well. A study by anthropologist Kate Fox showed that women view gambling negatively, while men hold a slightly positive view. The study goes on to state that women are more likely to avoid smoking, wear a seat belt, and brush their teeth.

Men's willingness to take risk in an effort to beat the market, however, is sadly misplaced. Academic research reveals that a mere one out of three professional managers beat their benchmark over five years, with the odds dramatically decreasing over a ten-year time span. Women seem more able to grasp this reality, and invest accordingly by taking a longer-term approach.

A WEE BIT IMPATIENT

During the financial collapse of 2008, one nationwide survey revealed that one in eight men—as opposed to one in forty women—made trades during the collapse in an effort to reevaluate, change paths, or find a new strategy for future growth. Ms. Fox, whose research revealed that women are more patient and less impulsive with their investing, confirmed such switches in investment approach. This results in a less active approach with fewer transaction fees, lower tax friction, and, as the science confirms, better returns.

WHY ASK FOR DIRECTIONS?

Most everyone seems to have a tale of a male driver being lost and unwilling to stop and ask for directions. Whether myth or fact, Fox's research revealed that when it comes to finances, women are more apt to admit ignorance and reach out for help. While both men and women lack knowledge when it comes to certain financial products, women have a higher likelihood of asking for more information and clarification. More facts result in better investment decisions and performance.

By stepping out of the testosterone-laden sandbox of active money management and resisting the impulse to compete to win, men can take a page out of the playbook of their gender counterparts. Simple global diversification, low-cost and tax-efficient indexing, and commitment to maintaining allocations over the long haul are great building blocks for portfolio success.

Ride Your Investments Toward Peace of Mind

(FEBRUARY 6, 2010)

"Love Rollercoaster," sung by the Ohio Players in the 1970s and popularized by the Red Hot Chili Peppers, laments that love has its ups and down. Over the past decade, investors have felt as though they are on an amusement ride, but unfortunately it is more like Disney's Tower of Terror. When it comes to investing, your emotions can run amok as you begin to worry that your portfolio has jumped the tracks and is headed for a devastating end. As your portfolio moves with the vicissitudes of the market, your emotions can drive investment decisions that are actually quite harmful. This emotional influence, or behavior gap, explains why the average investor substantially underperforms the average investment by 10 percent.

The sections that follow look at the important area of behavioral finance and reveal the importance of keeping your emotions out of the investment equation. By committing to the MarketRiders plan and rebalancing when instructed, you will be able to set aside the destabilizing force of emotion and do what is best for your retirement and family. Instead of worry, you will have peace of mind knowing that the ride you are on has a happy ending.

The Greed Gland

(MAY 28, 2011)

Silicon Valley was facing the beginnings of another tech bubble. In times like these, sticking to an asset allocation model is harder because it seems that everyone else is making a killing. A little perspective as to why asset allocation works had to be reinforced.

There must be an undiscovered gland in the human body. We know it is there. We call it the "greed gland." Wikipedia says a gland is an "organ in an animal's body that synthesizes a substance for release such as hormones…often into the bloodstream or into cavities inside the body or its outer surface." When we hear that others are profiting from an investment and getting wealthier and we're not, this gland starts excreting the envy chemical. Envy is an emotion that "occurs when a person lacks another's (perceived) superior quality, achievement or possession and either desires it or wishes that the other lacked it."

Greed glands were on fire last week when LinkedIn went public. Maybe this was your mental ticker tape: "How could I have gotten in on that action? Why did I miss LinkedIn and now Yandex? When Zynga, Facebook, and Foursquare offer IPOs, how can I get shares? How about all those Silicon Valley geeks getting rich again? Are social networking companies going to become another tech bubble? Will I profit from it? Am I going to sit on my hands? Maybe I'll just buy LinkedIn now at ninety dollars. It is a good company. I use it. It will eventually go higher."

DON'T HEED THE GREED

That's the greed gland talking. There' s no doubt that LinkedIn is a fantastic business! This professional network has over 90 million members will soon have revenues of $400 million. Its model has all the wonderful characteristics of a web-based business, but it is likely not worth anywhere near $9 billion today.

Fortunes have been lost buying great businesses at the wrong price. Fortunes have been made buying bad businesses at great discounts (Warren Buffett called it "cigar-butt" investing).

The greed grand and its secretion of envy will drive you to buy when you feel you are being left behind. Those who fall prey to it become speculators. It might be wise to clip the following words and read them when your greed gland starts convulsing: "Stay aboard for the long haul."

CAPITALISM 101 SAYS THE OWNER WILL BE PAID

When you invest or loan your money to companies that operate in our capitalistic system, you as an owner will be paid. Over the time period that retirement investors care about, say twenty or so years, that return has been in the 8 percent to 10 percent range. Think of capitalism as a train. If you get on it, your money will grow because the system demands a return on invested capital. Over the journey, the train will slow, backtrack, or speed up, but it will keep chugging along. Eighteen years ago, in 1993, you could have bought the S&P 500 in a newly minted product called SPY (the first ETF) for thirty-three dollars. Today SPY is worth four times that—$132. You'd have made no decisions, clipped some dividends, and paid minimal taxes without breaking a sweat. No CNBC, no commentary, little anxiety. Just ownership of a small piece of American capitalism.

WE CALL IT MARKETRIDERS, NOT MARKET JUMPERS

If you get off the train, you become a speculator, thinking you can get farther than those who are on the train. Speculating is thrilling and cures the temporary itch of the greed gland, but there are two problems that few overcome. First, you pay taxes on the gains, so your winnings are automatically cut by one-third to one-half. You have to run even harder and faster. Second, all speculators make mistakes. Few investors like to talk about investment mistakes, but everyone makes them. Every seasoned professional investor knows that avoiding and limiting the inevitable mistake is the single most important characteristic of investment success.

If you think you have a talent for buying LinkedIn and other IPO shares and sprint in front of the train, you may get a town or two ahead this year, but sooner or later, you will make a mistake. You'll buy too high on an oversized bet and feel pain as your losses pile up. Like all speculators, the train will pass or run over you at some point in the next ten or twenty years. Your friends will be having fun on the train and you'll be road kill. Please, just stay on the train, buy yourself a drink, and enjoy the ride.

Three Factors That Can Destroy Your Retirement

(OCTOBER 16, 2010)

While many retirement investors have felt tempted to flip Wall Street the middle finger in recent years, Italian artist Maurizio Cattelan took this impulse to a new level. In a highly publicized event, Cattelan created a bold sculpture called L.O.V.E., an eleven-meter-tall marble middle finger that has been strategically placed at the entrance to the Milan Stock Exchange by the city council of this fashionable Italian city.

Intended or not, the controversial artist successfully tapped into a deep reservoir of investor sentiment. His sculpture, though criticized by stock exchange representatives, has been met with public praise. While it remains a mystery as to what L.O.V.E. stands for, it is clear that when it comes to investing, many investors aren't feeling the love.

As good as it may feel to flip the finance industry the finger, it provides little salve for a damaged retirement portfolio.

Additionally, researchers have demonstrated that bringing emotions into portfolio management is directly linked to poor returns. In fact, the burgeoning field of behavioral finance has demonstrated several areas where investors would do well to control their emotions.

Three of the most significant emotional land mines identified by behavioral finance experts are recency, loss aversion, and overconfidence:

1. RECENCY.

This is the psychological tendency to overweight the recent past when reviewing historical information. The investment effect can be devastating. Apple and Google have been hot in recent months, so investors pile in. Sure, everyone remembers the collapse of the tech bubble in 2002, but this time is different—or so the deluded investor thinks.

Solution: The way to overcome recency is to follow the example of an institutional investor whose methodology is informed by deep and long-reaching historical time frames. The result is a portfolio built around very specific asset allocation goals. By defining your target allocation and committing to that focus, you can overcome the psychological impulse to follow the latest fad.

2. LOSS AVERSION.

Behavioral finance experts have revealed that investors feel twice the pain from loss as they do the pleasure of gain. When an investor's portfolio grows by 30 percent in a year, he definitely feels good, but when that same investor's portfolio dropped by 30 percent in 2007, he likely felt that his financial world had come to an end.

Solution: By acknowledging the physiological influence of loss aversion, you can begin to tame this emotional beast. Begin by taking your defined asset allocation and committing to disciplined rebalancing. When an asset class is running to the moon, a firm commitment to rebalancing will help you capture gains and prepare for future market shifts, which the science of investing suggests will surely come.

3. OVERCONFIDENCE.

Another discovery is that all human beings have an innate tendency to believe they can outwit the markets. This superman effect can lead investors to believe they can leap normal investment returns in a single bound. The result is overtrading, getting married to a single security, or abandoning a predefined allocation. Worse yet, some investors who act on overconfidence will experience short-lived success, deepening their faith in their own ability. Unfortunately, a small fraction of investors can sustain these superpowers for any length of time, and sooner or later they end up crashing to the earth as the kryptonite of highly efficient markets win the day.

Solution: A great elixir for overconfidence is a good dose of historical reality. Add to your investing an ongoing commitment to reviewing the history of equity markets. Draw upon examples of equities and sectors that were at one moment highly celebrated but quickly turned awry. In 1999, Enron was universally praised as an energy giant. One year later, it was toast. History is replete with examples where investors could not see the cliff around the next turn.

Instead of giving Wall Street the middle finger, embrace a disciplined approach to your retirement investing. Be aware of subliminal power of recency, loss aversion, and overconfidence. By committing to a clear asset allocation and disciplined rebalancing, you will outwit your emotions and feel that often-elusive investment love.

Zen and the Art of Retirement Investing

(NOVEMBER 27, 2010)

It has been proven that most active investors who struggle to outperform the market find that over time, their machinations and efforts were all for naught. A recent study showed that these efforts don't help one's happiness, either. On this Thanksgiving weekend, we present a few studies that address the connection between happiness and money.

A Gallup World Poll of 132 nations and over 136,000 respondents revealed that the United States, though the richest nation on Earth, is losing out to poorer nations when it comes to personal contentment. Latin American countries trounced the United States in day-to-day happiness, even though their income levels fell far short.

Why? According to the study, after basic human needs are addressed, happiness appears to increase based on rewarding relationships and a strong sense of community, not greater wealth.

Researchers found two categories of happiness that correlate to wealth. The first relates to our overall assessment of our life and is rooted in how we compare ourselves with our peers. We tend to establish an internal accomplishment rating such that the greater our wealth, the more our satisfaction depends on our perception of how we are doing relative to others in our world.

The second type of happiness was day-to-day contentment, measured by behaviors such as laughing, smiling, joy, and what researchers call social-psychological well being. Shockingly, any income increase over $75,000 a year had no impact on day-to-day contentment.

One of the more revealing findings was that the more time we spend thinking about money, the lower our happiness rating. When researchers exposed subjects to pictures of large amounts of dollars or euros, their savory rating (a measurement of how good the subject felt toward images) substantially decreased.

When we sense that our life is financially secure, we score higher in terms of day-to-day happiness. As Dr. Ed Diener of the University of Illinois pointed out, one individual may have a motor home while another owns a mansion. If the person with the motor home feels secure that it will never be taken, then his happiness rating will be higher than the individual who is fearful of losing a mansion. This security principle underscores the importance of living within our budget and not putting retirement capital at unnecessary risk.

These studies have clear implications for investing styles and underscore the value of passive asset allocation over stock picking and active forms of management. Active management requires increasing risk in the never-ending search for increasing returns. Index investing across a variety of asset classes lowers risk and provides much greater stability to our portfolios.

Could adopting our MarketRiders investment philosophy increase happiness? Using an asset allocation strategy with index funds or ETFs frees your time for more important things in life. When you know your money is diversified and your assets are safe, you can leave your computer behind and get busy with the truly valuable things in life. You'll think less about your money and more about the people around you. And contrary to what some might believe, most friends and family members don't want to hear about your recent stock or option conquest.

Can't Buy Me Love

(DECEMBER 25, 2010)

If you have ever felt confused about the relationship between money and happiness, you're not alone. Even the Beatles were torn over the subject, declaring in one famous song, "You can't buy me love," and lamenting in another, "But your lovin' don't pay my bills. Now give me money. That's what I want."

Gallup researchers have helped clear up this conundrum through a series of worldwide polls. The results have once again stirred interest in this ancient debate, answering with the discovery that annual earnings over $75,000 fail to add to an individual's happiness. Thinking less about money and financial security, as opposed to net worth, also plays heavily into an individual's happiness.

1. Appreciation of assets, depreciation of enjoyment. Daniel Gilbert from the University of Liege took the Gallup findings further through his research into what is now known as the experience-stretching hypothesis. His studies demonstrate that when individuals experience greater luxuries, their ability to appreciate the simpler pleasures in life decreases incrementally. These findings put an ironic twist on the American dream of wealth and the good life. As Gilbert points out, just when people have finally gathered the discretionary income to enjoy the finer things, they subconsciously train themselves to lose appreciation for the more common, daily pleasures.

Jonah Lehrer of *Wired* commented on these findings, stating, "Strangely, the more we indulge our desires, we strangely end up simply needing more. Discovering satisfaction—the ability to appreciate all we already have, is revolutionary."

Before you jump on the money-can't-buy-me-love bandwagon, however, it is important to note that the findings revealed that money *can* be useful in promoting well being in several surprising ways. Here are four ways money can buy you happiness:

2. Invest in index funds using asset allocation. Beware of the torrent of wealth managers pitching Yoda-like prognostications, technical analysis wizardry, or insider stock tips. The Wall Street machine seeks to appeal to your greed glands and lure you into its complicated web of high fees and high stress. These active investment strategies fall short both financially and psychologically. Low-cost indexing, asset allocation, and regular portfolio rebalancing will empower you to reject the greed mantra and free your mind for the more important activities.

3. Give to charity. Charitable giving has been shown to improve a person's sense of happiness. When people free up money to support a cause they believe in, their happiness rating increases. When you determine your asset allocation, you may want to practice the discipline of carving out some predetermined portion of your earnings for charitable causes. Adding this giving principle to your portfolio's allocation will provide an excellent return to your sense of well being.

4. Invest in personal growth. When money is spent on personal or professional growth, an individual's overall sense of well being increases. Graduate studies, counseling, and other forms of development seem to pay great dividends in personal satisfaction.

5. Allocate to "memory capital." Money may not be able to buy you love, but according to research, it can buy you great life memories. Researches call "memory capital" money spent creating outstanding experiences that will be savored over a lifetime. Such memories are revisited by individuals throughout the seasons of their lives and deliver an excellent psychological annuity.

In the end, research affirms what many intrinsically know: materialism has its limitations, and money should be used for retirement planning as well as for living. While global diversification through index funds and ETFs will aid retirement goals, allocating to charity, personal growth, and memory creation are also essential parts of a well-diversified life.

Retirement's New Normal

(FEBRUARY 12, 2011)

Recent research reveals that early retirement may not be the panacea many hope for. A slew of negative health effects have been correlated to early retirement, starting with memory decline. Unfortunately, mental exercises don't seem to help. Lisa Berkman of Harvard's Center for Population and Development states, "If you do crosswords or Sudoku, you get better at crosswords and Sudoku. You don't get better at cognitive behavior in life."

WORK LONGER, LIVE LONGER

Stanford's Center on Longevity discovered that maintaining the rigors of work actually keeps people functioning optimally. Richard Suzman of the National Institute on Aging says, "It may be the mental rigors, the social engagement, or even an aerobic component of work itself." Whatever the exact reason, getting out of bed each morning to face the workday creates a healthier and happier you.

It has also been noted by many of the world's great religions that humanity was created to be productive and live with a sense of purpose. Whether due to science or religion, work seems to benefit the human psyche. Retirees are the societal group most vulnerable to becoming restless and struggling with depression. "Only when we're retired do we discover what we've lost," says Christopher Sharpley, professor of psychology at the University of New England. "Immediately after retirement, there's a strong upsurge in well-being for the first six or so months, commonly known as the honeymoon period. After one or two years, there's a decrease in well-being, which can often turn into serious depression."

WORK GETS AN UPGRADE TO "HOLD"

Maybe work isn't as bad as we have been led to believe. A University of Chicago study revealed the influence of the prevailing cultural stereotype that work is bad and leisure is good. Researchers gave men and women of various ages and occupations a pager that would randomly beep eight times a day. They were each required to keep a log of their emotional state when the pager went off. When at work, 54 percent of respondents reported feeling "strong, creative, motivated, active, and positive." When away from work, a mere 18 percent noted these same positive emotions. When asked how they felt about work, however, the overwhelming majority of respondents said they would rather not be at work, but engaged in leisure activities.

These findings and others call into question the institution of retirement itself. Strangely, retirement wasn't a cultural concept until the 1880s, when Germany introduced the institution into its social structure. Before that time, people worked until death—a concept that may seem like a terrible plight to some, but that research is showing to have substantial benefit.

HOW WELL IS NOT WORKING ACTUALLY WORKING?

Today baby boomers are creating a new normal for retirement by scaling back on work hours while staying professionally engaged. Whether through consulting, reduced-hours agreements with their employer, or branching out as "seniorprenuers" by starting new business ventures, increasing numbers of seniors are finding an enjoyable work and life balance. The new retirement is no longer trading work for leisure, but trading work you no longer want to do for work you love to do, at the rate you want to do it.

When you look at the facts, it becomes compelling to reject the idea of traditional retirement. Whether you embrace the tenets of ancient religions, which state that humanity was designed to live purposefully, or to science, which shows that unused systems run down and go dormant, the results are clear: use it or lose it.

Analysis Paralysis: Three Ways Investors Can Break Free

(FEBRUARY 26, 2011)

Since March 2, 2009, a significant investor demographic has been frozen on the sidelines, while the S&P 500 has soared skyward by more than 95 percent. To get a sense of how much cash left the market and headed for the sidelines, a September 2009 Bloomberg study reported that record levels of bank deposits and money market funds reached a shocking $9.55 trillion—enough to buy all the companies in the S&P 500 at the time.

How can investors suffering from paralysis of analysis break free and participate in the markets? Here are three approaches to consider:

1. JUMP INTO THE MARKET.

Jumping into the markets with a Dow average north of 12,000 may feel akin to jumping into Lake Michigan for the annual Polar Bear Plunge—in other words, crazy. But before you write off the idea, step back and consider the possible wisdom of this approach.

Wading into these frigid waters becomes more rational if you do so clothed in the warmth of a truly globally diversified portfolio. By adding US, foreign-developed, and emerging market stocks, commodities, US Treasuries, foreign and corporate debt, TIPS, and more to your portfolio, you stand largely protected from your worst fears. Additionally, disciplined rebalancing will allow you to do what few investors have the true grit to pull off—trim winners and buy losers, thereby reducing risk and positioning your portfolio for future market shifts.

Investors should not lose sight of individual time horizons. If a retirement investor has a time horizon of ten years or more, a 10 percent downside move in the markets will not adversely affect that investor's retirement dreams. Eventually, markets will sort themselves out and offer rewards to those who participate in their efforts.

2. DOLLAR-COST AVERAGE INTO THE MARKET.

Jumping into the markets isn't for everyone. That is why advisers have been recommending the practice of dollar-cost averaging for years. The idea behind dollar-cost averaging is that the investor will purchase fewer shares when prices are high but more when prices are low by investing a fixed amount of money at regular intervals. This will eventually drive down the average cost per share. Dollar-cost averaging is a time-honored investment technique, and it helps prevent investors from investing large amounts of money at the wrong time.

The challenge of dollar-cost averaging is the potentially negative effects of transaction costs related to each trade. These effects can largely be minimized, however, if you employ quality exchange-traded funds that trade for free at brokers such as Charles Schwab, Fidelity, and Vanguard. The approach does require discipline and a predetermined plan, but it can prove to be an effective cure for investor paralysis.

3. "PUT" YOUR WAY INTO THE MARKET.

Selling puts to move into a stock position is a sophisticated trading technique that requires education and diligence. If used wisely, however, selling puts can be an effective way to move from the sidelines and into a stock you are already planning to buy.

When you sell a naked put, someone is paying you to enter into a stock position you already intend to own. If the put expires worthless and fails to hit your strike price, you simply collect on the value of the put, allowing you to pocket the profit and write a new put for the future. If the stock hits your strike price, you then own the stock you intended to buy all along, but were paid a premium along the way in the form of the put. If the market crashes and your stock goes dramatically down, you are forced into the stock at your strike price and will lose money—but only money you would have lost if you had simply bought the stock outright.

This sophisticated trading technique is risky, but for the educated and astute, it can help you move from the sidelines back into the market. It is extremely important to do your research before employing this technique.

Breaking free of the paralysis of analysis is essential if an investor wants to enter and benefit from the eventual growth of economies and markets. A globally diversified and rebalanced portfolio will provide protection and participation in the market's growth. Whether you jump in, wade in, or get clever with puts, getting in is a good thing for long-term investors.

Managing Your Portfolio By Managing Your Mind

(JULY 1, 2011)

You might be familiar with Homer's epic tale of Ulysses and the sirens. The mythical sirens lived on rocky islands in the middle of the sea, where they sang such beautiful melodies that passing sailors could not resist their call. Sailors would inevitably steer their boats toward these melodies or even jump into raging waters to get closer, always with the same result—disaster.

Ulysses possessed uncommon wisdom. He knew that his journey required sailing past the sirens, but he wanted to hear their call. He knew that doing so would render him incapable of rational thought, so he put wax in his sailors' ears so that they could not hear. They tied him to the mast so that he could not jump into the sea. He ordered them not to change course under any circumstances, and to keep their swords upon him to attack him if he broke free of his bonds.

Upon hearing the sirens' song, Ulysses was driven temporarily insane and struggled to break free so that he might join them, but his forethought and thorough planning worked. Modern psychological research has revealed that Ulysses was on to something when it comes to managing the human psyche, which translates well to managing a retirement account. Turn a deaf ear when the sirens call. Tie yourself to the mastery of passive investing.

MISSED PROFITS: THE DOPE ON DOPAMINE

Dr. Read Montague recently uncovered groundbreaking insight on dopamine neurons. He gave subjects $100 each to invest in the stock market, supplying information on market trends and conditions from actual but not-yet-revealed historic market periods. The subjects participated in twenty-four rounds of investing—and got to keep their earnings—while Montague monitored the dopamine response in their brains.

What did Montague learn? When an investor placed a bet with 10 percent of a portfolio and saw investments shoot up in value, the dopamine neuron pattern revealed a fixation—not on the winnings, but on the missed profits, as the investor's neurons calculated the possible returns relative to the actual returns.

What did the subjects do in the following investment round? They wagered more and more of their portfolios in search of the profits they had previously missed, in an effort to drown their regret with pleasurable dopamine. Interestingly, the longer the investment provided returns, the more the subjects grew in confidence that they had figured out the winning formula, forming a type of investment bubble that would end in utter surprise when the markets corrected and the bubble burst.

Another modern neuroscientist, David Eagleman, provided some additional research on the brain and investing. In his recent book *Incognito: The Secret Lives of the Brain*, Eagleman reveals that the conscious mind is not at the center of the brain's action, but rather at the periphery. Our conscious decision-making activity is often directed by a staggeringly complex neural subpopulation.

IMMEDIATE GRATIFICATION VERSUS LONG-TERM RESULTS

One population looks at chocolate-chip cookies and sees pleasure, another sees a high-energy source for survival, and yet another sees an hour on the treadmill at the gym. An unconscious democratic process unfolds in our minds that results in a split-second decision to eat or not eat the cookie. While the cookie debate is fairly easily understood, the subconscious process becomes much more complex and subversive in areas such as finance. That is why Mr. Eagleman recommends that we make well-devised plans during moments of psychological clarity to help guide our minds in the important areas of life.

When it comes to portfolio management, many everyday investors do not have clear and strong investment principles to guide them. They are left to face to the sirens of greed, fear, jealousy, and a host of other anxieties fomented by media, society, and Wall Street that eventually lead to undisciplined and irrational investment decisions.

In contrast, professional portfolio managers work within strict asset allocation models that are rarely changed and only with strict review and committee decisions. Such institutional money managers know how to block out the sirens and stay the course.

MAKE A PACT WITH YOURSELF AND YOUR MONEY

Ulysses was wise enough to foresee the temptations ahead and designed a plan to stay the course. Psychologists call this mental discipline a Ulysses pact. Do you have enough psychological clarity to know that down the road you, too, will want to abandon your investment ship in search of siren songs? Market swings, stock tips, bubbles, and stories of remarkable profits at cocktail parties will leave those bereft of a portfolio Ulysses pact tossed about by temptation and apt to dive headlong into disaster.

The sirens' songs will be strong. By forming a clear and rational portfolio allocation plan and committing to stay the course over time through rigorous rebalancing, you can avoid the shoals and sail on toward retirement safety.

Experts Speak

"There is a secret psychology of money. Most people don't know about it. That's why most people never become financially successful. A lack of money is not the problem; it is merely a symptom of what's going on inside of you."

—T. HARV EKER, AUTHOR AND PERSONAL FINANCE EXPERT

"Behavioral finance is the study of the influence of psychology on the behavior of financial practitioners and the subsequent effect on markets."

—MARTIN SEWELL, ECONOMIST

"Behavioral economics combines the twin disciplines of psychology and economics to explain why and how people make seemingly irrational or illogical decisions when they spend, invest, save, and borrow money.

—GARY BELSKY, THOMAS GILOVICH, AUTHORS, *BUSINESS & ECONOMICS* (1999)

"The Efficient Market Hypothesis survives the challenges from behavior finance research. Although market inefficiencies emerge, over time these anomalies tend to disappear as rationality inevitably wins the day."

—GARY SCHMIEG, ECONOMIST

"The game of speculation is the most uniformly fascinating game in the World. But it is not a game for the stupid, the mentally lazy, the man of inferior emotional balance, or for the get-rich-quick adventurer. They will die poor."

—JESSE LIVERMORE, AUTHOR

Afterword

After the love (of Wall Street) is gone…

We hope this book has helped educate you on the deleterious effects of fees that lurk within your portfolios, strangling its growth. You don't have to let Wall Street pick your pocket. Rather, by pulling back, you too can rebuild your portfolio around the simple concepts of low-cost asset allocation, index investing and disciplined rebalancing. If you need help, check out our growing community of investors at MarketRiders (www.marketriders.com). Here's to great investing!

—Mitch & Steve

About the Authors

Most people still believe that the best way to manage their money is to either pick stocks themselves or pay for trusted advice from investment advisers, brokers, or mutual fund managers so that they can "beat the market." But for years, sophisticated families and elite institutions have achieved superior returns with a very different method of investing that was developed by Economics and Finance Nobel Laureates.

Their secret involves implementing a sophisticated asset allocation strategy with a globally diversified portfolio, keeping investment costs low and rebalancing their portfolios as markets ebb and flow. Because they don't pick stocks and they don't try to time the market, they have less stress than active traders. They are investing, not gambling.

The authors created MarketRiders, an internet-based online service used by thousands of do-it-yourself investors that makes it easy to use these methods. MarketRiders subscribers receive a customized, globally diversified, low-cost ETF or index fund portfolio, created by world experts. Members then buy their portfolio at their own online broker. MarketRiders monitors these portfolios 24/7 and sends email alerts when it is time to rebalance.

STEPHEN R. BECK

Stephen R. Beck is serial entrepreneur who started several successful companies over his twenty-five-year career. Prior to MarketRiders, Steve served as general partner of Integrity Partners, a venture capital firm in Danville, California. He was a founding investor and board member of Baidu, considered the Google of China, and worked closely with other portfolio companies including Hydration Technologies, a pioneer in water purification technologies. Steve was on the founding team of C2B Technologies in 1996 and, after its sale to Inktomi in 1998, he ran business development and pioneered dozen of landmark partnerships. In the 1980s, Steve cofounded CCS, which grew to become the world's largest action sports mail-order and e-commerce business and was acquired by Alloy Inc. He holds a bachelor degree from Cal Poly San Luis Obispo.

MITCHELL TUCHMAN

Mitchell Tuchman is a Silicon Valley veteran with more than twenty-six years of experience in venture capital, public finance, strategy, and technology. Prior to MarketRiders, Mitch was a subadviser for microcap technology investments for Apex Capital, LLC. From 1997 to 2001, Mitch invested in and advised venture funds focusing primarily on Internet. He began his career at Atari, Inc. and served as an operating executive for several Silicon Valley companies, leading them through strategic transformations. He served as director for several public companies, including Phoenix Technologies and Kintera. Mitch holds a bachelor of science in business administration from Boston University and an MBA from Harvard Business School.

www.ingramcontent.com/pod-product-compliance
Lightning Source LLC
Chambersburg PA
CBHW020206200326
41521CB00005BA/260
* 9 7 8 0 6 1 5 6 0 8 3 1 0 *